THE ENIGMA

James Clemon
and
Gilles Monif

iUniverse, Inc.
Bloomington

The Enigma

iUniverse books may be ordered through booksellers or by contacting:

iUniverse
1663 Liberty Drive
Bloomington, IN 47403
www.iuniverse.com
1-800-Authors (1-800-288-4677)

ISBN: 978-1-4502-9167-5 (sc)
ISBN: 978-1-4502-9165-1 (e)
ISBN: 978-1-4502-9166-8 (dj)

Library of Congress Control Number: 2011908291

Printed in the United States of America

iUniverse rev. date: 10/18/2011

PREFACE

I met Evelyn Riley during her community service assignment at a primary drug treatment center in Omaha, Nebraska. Her supervisor told Mrs. Riley, mother of two children, that a professor from Creighton University School of Medicine was going to be conducting a research study and was looking for someone to assist him at the treatment center. She asked permission to apply.

Most of the interview focused on the position's requirements, patient rights, and ethics. At a certain point in the interview, I asked Evelyn about her expectations and goals. At no time did the conversation venture into why she had gone to prison or why she was on probation.

Over time, trust developed between us. Finally one afternoon, she was told that I wanted to see her in the clinic superintendent's office. When she sat down I asked her who she was. Evelyn replied "Bandit Riley." I did not accept the answer and repeated the question. The answer came back the same. Then, I rephrased the question. "What are you?" This time the answer came back: "A man trapped in a woman's body." I got the answer already implied by her facial hair pattern and body language.

That is when he told me the first part of his story.

The development of trust gained me access to his story and an introduction to a fantastic lawyer named Patrick J. Bailey who had been his trial attorney. Patrick furnished me with the trial transcript. I encouraged Bandit to write his life story. Bandit was a gifted writer, but he died before finishing it. He wanted his story to reach out with a message of hope to those who have shared a similar fate: being trapped in the other sex's body.

Bandit's story was worth telling; but to tell it well, I needed to turn to a gifted friend, James Clemon, who had been a senior editorial writer for the Omaha World Herald, and asked him to take Bandit's story to the next level.

If Bandit's story were a work of fiction, it would challenge credibility. While liberties have been taken with some of the peripheral individuals involved, *The Enigma* is anything but a work of fiction. The murder trial per se and its outcome are factually based.

Both Jim Clemon and I, being former military officers, were impressed by the military justice system. A mistake was made but corrected. In 1983, the U.S. Army recognized the potential of mis-sex imprinting occurring *in utero*. In so doing, it demonstrated a level of understanding and compassion that society has yet to achieve three decades later.

DEDICATION

To Cecilia Riley

ACKNOWLEDGMENT:

The authors thank Patrick J. Bailey, Esq. for his gracious support in providing the trial transcript and encouragement.

CONTENTS

PROLOGUE

"In the military, there are a lot of reasons straights go the other way. The service attracts a fair percentage of men who either physically or psychologically abuse their women.

You also have females who have been neglected as children. Then, along comes a woman who gives one hundred and ten percent of caring and attention and initially asks nothing in return. When she later asks a sexual favor, they may feel obligated — if not just downright horny.

I guess I'd have to say that for most part, same-sex relationships occur for the same reasons as for anyone else — love, companionship, and acceptance. Sexual satisfaction is important, sometimes even very important, but it's not number one. It wasn't with Denise.

Being with Denise was the only thing that ever made sense in my life. She was the first person that I felt comfortable with. In my teens, I didn't like having regular sex. I thought sleeping around with boys was just something a girl did. Even then, I wanted to be a boy. Now, I want to be a man!

If you're born poor, like I was, too often you lived in the rain. If you're poor and black, the rain can be a storm. By my birth, my storm became a hurricane due to forces I did not understand. I am living my life in a flesh-and-bone prison. In what is my physical world, I do not fit in and it is tearing me apart.

My mother once told me, "Child, if the person that you're sleeping with don't make you happy just the way you are, find someone that will." Denise made me very happy. I didn't want to ever lose her. She's the only person who accepted me as a man in a woman's body and, in so doing, delivered me from the hell within."

"Bandit" Riley

Forever

The moonlight from an open window silhouettes two female figures, one on top of the other, on a high, king-sized four poster bed.

"Do you love me?" the stockier-built female asks as she lifts the upper part of her torso with her arms.

"Yes, you know that," replies from the more full-bodied female on the bottom.

"I mean forever."

"Yes, Forever!" The two silhouettes merge into one.

Omaha, Nebraska
12 May 1959

Now the pains are coming every ten minutes. From the birth of her two previous children, Cecilia Riley knows that today will be the day. Cecilia has a light yellow-brown complexion, hazel eyes and reddish hair, reflective of a prior mixing of white and black genes.

Suddenly, Cecilia doubles over. Time stands still for a fraction of a second. The contraction that has just passed is much stronger. The pain tells her that the birth will be sooner than she thought. Holding the back of a chair for support, she calls to her youngest son, "Davie, go get your father."

At the hospital, Cecilia is taken immediately to Labor & Delivery. There, her pelvic hair is shaved. The contractions are now less than two minutes apart.

Dr. James Ristack hurriedly enters the room.

The nurse whispers, "The fetal heart rate is too slow."

Quickly assuming a position at the bottom of the delivery table, he deftly inserts two fingers into the vaginal opening. "The cord is wrapped around the baby's neck."

When Cecilia Riley awakens, a nurse is placing a tray by her bed. She calls out, "Nurse, what did I have?"

Quickly, the reply comes back, "A baby"

"No, no! What did I have?"

Each time Cecelia asks, the reply is the same: "A baby."

After what seems an eternity, Dr. Ristack appears at her bedside holding an isolate. "Here's your baby," he says "alive and breathing. It was being strangled by the umbilical cord and didn't breathe for a few minutes. The good news is that there doesn't appear to be any damage."

Cecilia looks into the isolate and counts ten fingers and ten toes before she drifts back into a medication-induced sleep.

At 8:30 a.m. the next morning, she awakens to a familiar voice. "Honey, we have a beautiful baby girl. What shall we call her?"

Excited, Cecilia sits up in bed. "Finally, a girl! We'll call her Evelyn: Evie for short. When we get home, we'll invite all the family…"

Her husband interrupts quickly. "It'll be a few days before she comes home."

"David, is anything wrong with the baby?"

He doesn't answer immediately, but walks to the window and looks out. "No, they just want to watch her for a few days."

Cecilia Riley has been heavily medicated during her hospital stay. She is oblivious to the passage of time during which a meeting is held involving the hospital administrators, the hospital's lawyers, Reverend Riley, Dr. Ristack, the labor and delivery staff on call that night and all of the newborn nursery staff. The subject of that meeting, as well as the entire newborn file of Evelyn Riley, is to be sequestered from hospital records and sealed by court order.

What transpired during her birth at St. Joseph's Hospital in Omaha, Nebraska, will remain a carefully maintained secret until, charged with first-degree murder, Evelyn Riley Davis stands trial for her life.

_____

LAS CRUSES, NEW MEXICO
10 APRIL 1983

Denise insists that they go to the nightclub where she is the disc jockey on weekends. Once inside the club,

Denise goes to her work and Evelyn joins a group of women that she and Denise party with.

Several hours pass, when Evelyn spies an attractive, well-dressed female by the name of Sabrina James at another table. Evelyn mentions to her cousin, Mindy, how nice Sabrina's outfit looks. Her cousin turns to Evelyn and says "send her a drink" Evelyn answers "I don't have any money left on my card."

"Not a problem," comes the reply.

When the drink gets to the table, the waitress says something to Sabrina. She gets up and walks over to the table and thanks Evelyn. Minutes later, Denise is at Sabrina's table. "If Evelyn bought you that drink and you like your health, don't drink it."

Shortly after her last session, Denise storms up to Evelyn. "That bitch is going around the club talking about what she is going to do to me." Grabbing Evelyn by the wrist, Denise begins looking for Sabrina. After a fifteen minute search, Denise is ready to give up. She tells Evelyn "My mascara is running. Let me go into the restroom and clean up before we leave."

The open door reveals Sabrina sitting in front on a large mirror, dolling up. Seeing Sabrina, Denise calls out, "Bandit, get your black ass in here and tell this bitch that you don't buy her a drink."

"I.. ...." Before Evelyn can respond completely, the fight begins. The two women are rolling on the floor ripping each other's clothes. Denise comes out on top. Sitting straddling Sabrina, Denise says, "You have a pretty face and Bandit likes it; but he won't like it after I'm done." With that Denise digs her fingernails into Sabrina's face.

Then Denise starts to choke Sabrina, until Sabrina's right fist makes contact with her jaw.

The commotion of the fight has attracted a small crowd at the doorway's threshold. Denise reaches back over her head and grabs a heavy ashtray. Before it can find its mark, Evelyn catches her arm. Other observers drag Denise off a badly shaken Sabrina James.

Outside the club, a very concerned Evelyn Davis turns to Denise and with a conflicted voice says, "With one dead body in the desert, we don't need another."

The night ends with the police making a report. On base, Evelyn is known as Evelyn Davis. Among her friends and in the lesbian clubs of Las Cruses and El Paso Texas, Evelyn Davis is known simply as Bandit. In the police report filed in Las Cruses, the name of one of the witnesses is listed as "Bandit".

Texas-New Mexico Border
8 April 1983

Snow flurries had fallen on parts of the White Sand Missile Range and Fort Bliss, leaving a light white dusting on the young woman lying on her side, one arm outstretched in a slight depression about 25 yards from the road. Her eyes are open. She is wearing a blue T-shirt and jeans, white socks, and white high-topped sneakers. Lingering gusts of cold wind blow her locks of long black hair across her face.

"What do I put down for age?"

Detective Ray Martinez of the El Paso Police Department steps back from the body. "Early twenties." The young highway patrolman writes it down.

Up on the elevated roadway, a drab olive sedan pulls up behind the two other cars parked on the shoulder of the two lane road. Two men get out: one a tall black soldier wearing an M.P. brassard. The other is a lithe, short, erect figure wearing cameo fatigues and a crisply starched field jacket. A colonel's eagle glitters on Mark Silverstine's Ridgeway cap.

Martinez inwardly grimaces. He has dealt with Colonel Mark Silverstine before when the activities of the El Paso P.D. and the White Sands M.P. have intersected. If pressed for a description of Fort Bliss's head cop, he would probably say "arrogant son-of-a-bitch".

They formally shake hands.

"So what have you got that brings the provost marshal out on a day like this?" Silverstine asks, gesturing towards the huddled body.

"A dead one. Young black female in her early twenties," replies Martinez. "Guys in a garbage truck were heading for the landfill over there and spotted her about 7:30 a.m. They got a radio in their truck and called their dispatcher. He called the highway patrol. They called us."

"Okay," Silverstine says, "but where does the Army come in?"

Martinez bends down and turns back the collar of the girl's T-shirt, exposing the size tag and a handwritten laundry tag reading, 4AM-3. "I think she's one of yours. We're not going to move the body until processing of the crime scene is totally finished. But for now, that tag looks like it came from the post laundry and when she is rolled over I'll bet that there'll be an Army logo on the front."

"Good call" acknowledges Silverstine. "That'd be a PX shirt, not uniform issue. A lot of our people wear them off-duty. What else?"

"We're looking at a homicide." Martinez pulls down one of the girl's lower eyelids. He points to several small purple irregularities on her conjunctivae and face. "Conjunctivae and skin petechiae -small amount of blood on the snow around the lower portion of her mouth- stains in the jeans indicating defecation, a superficial groove around her neck. Add it up: she was choked to death. If you want it in M.E. language: death due to ligature asphyxiation by strangulation."

Silverstine nods. "How long?"

"Judging by liver temperature, last night or early this morning. She was here before it started snowing. If you reach under the body and touch the front of her shirt, it's dry."

Martinez gestures to the crime scene. "There's no sign of a fight or struggle. Looks like she was killed somewhere else and dumped here."

Silverstine says to himself *'Murder. Victim probably military. No, certainly military-civilian law enforcement in play. We're in the El Paso city limits. God knows where she was killed or what happened.'*

He shakes his head and says out loud, "Til we find out what the jurisdiction is. I guess we'll do our old military-civilian cooperation routine again."

Martinez replies curtly, "You do yours and we'll do ours."

Silverstine turns and heads back to the warmth of his car, leaving a highway patrolman and the M.P. to fag the scene for the forensic team in transit from Fort Bliss.

As a random gust of wind sprinkles a few snowflakes over the corpse, the young M.P. looking at the body, says to himself, *"What a waste."*

WHITE SANDS MISSILE RANGE, FORT BLISS, NEW MEXICO
10 APRIL 1983

Ray Martinez has never been in the E Ring of the Pentagon, but after his first look at Colonel Mark Silverstine's office, he knows what it might be like. Flags, military memorabilia, photos of Silverstine with powerful figures make Silverstine's room either an ego shrine or a stage set to intimidate or both.

Though not intimidated by the Pattonesque décor, nevertheless, Martinez has to suppress an impulse from his own military service to come to attention and salute. He shakes Silverstine's extended hand and sits down across from him. "You said that you have something to show me?"

"Yes. On your end, your boys did a credible job with the crime scene." Silverstone taps a file on his desk that contains the two forensic reports with other documents.

"We got what is there," Martinez responds, pointing to the file. "But as you can see, it wasn't much: no footprints, no cigarette butts, no bottles, no weapons, and no tire track on the shoulder. Nothing that somebody dropped," responds Martinez

"Yes, I noted that" Silverstine says turning on a 30 percent smile, the kind that Martinez suspects he reserves for use on lieutenants and below. "Our people got a little more: in fact, quite a bit more."

Silverstine pushes a second file toward Martinez. "The victim is Specialist 4 Angela Kinney, age 23, assigned to the 62nd transport Company at Fort Bliss. She had a decent service record, but her private life is something else. Angela was no angel. Seems that she was a switch-hitter who did best from the left side of the plate."

"You mean a lesbian", interrupts Martinez.

"That is calling it a little tight. For now let's just say that she appears to be an individual with ambivalent sexual preferences."

"I thought the military had zero tolerance for gays."

"Well," Silverstine replies, "military policy and what really happens can sometimes be a little different. A lot depends on the circumstances, the command's philosophy. If somebody's doing their job, not making trouble, not getting in your face with it, some commanders just sort of look the other way. But when a problem arises that compromises the integrity of the U.S. Army, they have no option but to get hard-nosed."

Martinez is surprised that Silverstine is speaking so candidly. He had him pegged as being in the front rank of officers saying "Throw 'em out."

"Anyway," Silverstine continues, "that's really not why you're here." He slides another thick folder across the desk.

Martinez leafs through the preliminary pages that cover what he already knows. His attention becomes focused on the log of phone calls made from White Sands. One entry is highlighted in yellow marker. It records that a call had been made to the orderly room of Angela Kinney's unit at Fort Bliss, from a phone listed to an Alan C. Davis at White Sands. The date is four days after Kinney's body was found.

"This phone call to Fort Bliss, it's what put you onto Angela Kinney?"

"Not really," Silverstine says. "The first sergeant at the 62nd had already reported that a female soldier, one Angela Kinney, was being carried on the morning report as an AWOL. We got somebody from Bliss to come up and identify the body. It didn't take much to put it all together."

"Wouldn't have taken much to let us know sooner what was going on," Martinez thinks to himself.

As if he read the detective's mind, Silverstine says, upping his smile to 35 percent, "We decided we'd hold off bringing you in till we had more in place."

Martinez reads on. "Okay, This Denise Louise Rakes, whoever she is, gets into a fight with this Sabrina James, whoever she is, gets arrested and goes to court. She gets six months' probation, a hundred-dollar fine, and two weeks community service. What does this have to do with Angela Kinney getting strangled?"

"Just keep reading."

A page later, Martinez says, "This thing with Rakes and James in the bar was a catfight over another girl, a Specialist Evelyn Davis, so-called Bandit. A lesbian triangle?"

"You got it," Silverstine replies without emotion.

"I still don't get the connection with Kinney."

"You will. First, notice when it happened-April 10th. That would be three days after Kinney was killed."

Martinez flips to the next section of the file. The colonel's people had indeed been busy. Here are transcripts of interviews with soldiers at White Sands and Fort Bliss. They all point to a probable sexual relationship between the dead woman, Angela Kinney, and Evelyn Davis and between Davis and Rakes and other female soldiers.

"This looks like more than a triangle," Martinez mutters partially under his breathe. "It's a damn network."

"I wouldn't call it that," Silverstine replies. "A network implies some kind of order and organization. This thing is more like a free-for-all, a general grab-ass. This Davis woman, the central object of everybody's affections, seems to have a nickname or alias. Calls herself "Bandit Riley" and so do some of the others."

Standing to signal that it is time for Martinez to leave, Silverstine goes on: "I don't think I need to say that from the Army's point of view, we need to keep a tight lid on this as far as publicity is concerned. Messy and sensational are things the Army certainly does not need. This murder is the U.S. Army's problem. The El Paso police department is here for the mandated ride and nothing more!"

Silverstine escorts him to the door. Martinez stops and turning back into the office responds, "Right now, the media doesn't have anything except what was in the state trooper's initial report and what we found at the scene, and that isn't much. It's off the front page already. If they come back and bug me, I'll just refer them to you."

Now it's Silverstine's turn to stop for a second before answering. Obviously, he had hoped for something more conclusive. "No problem. We will handle that."

EL PASO, TEXAS
18 APRIL 1983

Detective Martinez sits on the corner of a desk in the Detective Bureau bullpen. In addition to Detectives Dominic Fallow and Reginald Carter, four uniformed police officers are present.

"This is the way it's going to go down. It's a joint deal: us and the Army. We're going to pick up two suspects and bring them here for questioning. They're both currently under surveillance. Sometime late this afternoon, the M.P.s will pick 'em up and take 'em in. We'll take over from there. Use the vans with the outside locks."

One of the uniformed policemen raises his hand.

"Back up a little bit. Why all the elaborate stuff? If this is some kind of big deal national security issue, I'd kinda like to know more about what's going on."

"That's fair enough," Martinez answers. "Here's the deal. The objects of our concern are two female suspects in a murder. One's a civilian, the other's military, stationed at White Sands. The victim was military: a woman."

"If this is the Army's mess, why are we doing the leg work"?

"The body was found in our jurisdiction. If the killing was done on the post, and it looks like it was, then our only involvement is what happened out where the body was dumped, and maybe anything else that might have happened on our turf. The Army has asked, just short of ordering us, to cooperate and that it be done by the book. Clear?"

"I guess so," the uniform policeman answers.

"Okay," Martinez resumes. "Here's what'll happen. There'll be two of you in each van. Each van takes one prisoner. Don't cuff 'em. They aren't arrested yet; they're just being brought here for questioning. Use the tape machines in the vans. Record everything you and they say. What I want you to do is start a conversation. Keep it light. Don't sound like you're interrogating them. Get 'em to relax and be as talkative as possible. Don't be too obvious about it.

The same policeman raises his hand again. "How are we supposed to do that if we don't know any more about it than we do?"

"There isn't much," Martinez says. "The victim's name was Angela Kinney. The way it looks now, at least to the Army, is that one or both of these two women strangled the victim in a house on White Sands Missile Range, then drove her out in the country and dumped her body.

Their names are Denise Rakes and Evelyn Davis. Davis is sometimes called Bandit."

Martinez nods towards a rangy, serious looking, blonde female M.P. officer standing in the back of the bullpen. "This is Lieutenant Carlson. Anything comes up that looks like a jurisdictional problem, she'll be on the radio network. Just use the code word, Illusion."

Referring to a pocket notebook, he adds, "The way this thing is supposed to be timed, you should get them here around seven or eight o'clock tonight. By the time we get' em processed in, it should be late enough on Sunday night that they probably won't be able to get a lawyer in to tell 'em to shut up. That isn't exactly in the true spirit of Miranda, but it does give us and the Army a little more elbow room"

Martinez stands up. "Just one more thing, see if you can tell which one is the butch and which one is the fem. Draw your own conclusions. The Army is real nervous. They are acting like they don't know how to handle it because of the lesbian angle. They want to keep everything under wraps. If something becomes unglued, we are being set up so that there'll be somebody the brass can dump on. Be damn careful that nothing comes unglued."

EL PASO, TEXAS
18 APRIL 1983

The pick-up teams reassemble in the bullpen at about
8:45 p.m. Officer John Blanchard is the first to speak.

"Denise Rakes is the fem and the other one, Evelyn
Davis, is the butch. We couldn't get much on the way
over here, but it looks pretty obvious. Davis has a butch
haircut. Her deep voice and the way she carries herself
speak to that conclusion. She seems very protective of
Rakes."

"Okay," Martinez says. "Now, we got Rakes in
Interrogation Room A and Davis in Room B. They haven't
had the chance to talk to each other, and that's the way
we'll keep it. Silverstine and the other M.P. types will be
watching Rakes through the one-way mirror. They want
us to focus on her first."

"Basically, we're to keep Davis on ice for them while
they see what shakes loose in the other room."

He points at one of the detectives, a short, gray-haired
black man. "While I talk with Davis, Carter, you take
the first shot at Rakes. This time you get to be the good
cop. Try to loosen her up. If that doesn't work, I'll take
a turn."

Martinez starts toward the door, then, pauses. "One
more thing, just between us civilians, this whole deal
doesn't smell real good. I still don't know exactly what
our Army buddies are up to, but the last thing we need is
for the El Paso P.D. to get set up in case the wheels come

off. So play a lot of CYA, and let's not gossip about this around the shop. Clear?"

Amid nods and grunts of consent, the meeting breaks up.

Carter loosens his tie as he goes into Interrogation A.

Reginald Carter had been the first black detective on the El Paso force. Twenty years and an extra forty pounds now understate the qualities that had given him that distinction.

"How ya doin'? My name is Reginald Carter. I'm a detective here with the EI Paso police"

He offers to shake hands, but Rakes does not uncross her arms. Carter can't help but be impressed with what a looker Rakes is: a finely chiseled face on top of a voluptuous body. Definitely visual candy.

Carter takes a chair directly across the table from Rakes.

"I know this is tough and maybe you don't know what's going on exactly. I'm here to help if I can. We think we know what happened that night between you and Evelyn and Angela Kinney, but if there's anything more you can tell us, it'll probably be good for both of you."

Rakes continues to sit, arms folded, staring at a spot on the wall over Carter's shoulder.

"I suppose that means you don't want to make a statement, right?" Carter asks.

"I don't have anything to say to you or anybody else," Rakes replies curtly.

"You can have a lawyer, you know. All you have to do is call."

"I don't know a lawyer. I thought you were supposed to get me one if I didn't have one."

Carter shrugs. "No, we can't do that, at least, not tonight. But I can bring in a phone and a phone book and you can look one up. That be alright?"

Carter takes Rakes' silence as a yes. He leaves the room, only to return minutes later with a phone and a directory. He plugs the phone in, puts the directory down on the table in front of Denise Rakes, and leaves.

The growing number of observers behind the one-way wall mirror watch as she spends a half an hour going through the Yellow Pages, dialing number after number. Finally she appears to reach an attorney who'll talk to her. She speaks for about five minutes, then hangs up the phone and pushes her chair back from the table.

Carter re-enters the interrogation room. "Any luck?"

"I talked to a lawyer."

"And?"

"And he said I wasn't charged with anything. I wasn't even officially under arrest yet, and I didn't have to talk to you. So I'm not going to."

Carter tries another line. "Well, that's all right. We don't have to talk about the case. We can just visit a little here. You know-how you're doing -who your people are that maybe we should notify."

Again, no response. "Maybe I can get you something, coffee or a soda?"

Rakes continues to sit staring at the same spot on the wall.

"Well, okay," Carter says "I guess I'm done. Good luck. You'll need it"

A half hour later, Martinez enters the room. He does not bother with any preliminaries, but stands directly in front of Rakes.

"We're done messing around, Denise. You can make it hard on yourself or you can confirm what we already know and maybe get a break. There isn't much of a way out. You and Davis and Angela Kinney went into that house that night and only two of you came out alive. One of you strangled her: maybe both. Either way, you're both going to be charged with murder in the first-degree."

Martinez lights a cigarette. He pointedly does not offer Rakes one.

"We suppose Davis will get an Army court-martial and you'll probably go on trial here in EI Paso. I don't know how the Army executes murderers, but in Texas we use a lethal injection. You ready for that? Or do you want to see if you can make it easy for yourself?"

"I told that other cop I'm not making any statement"

"Suit yourself. But maybe your friend doesn't see it that way. She's over in the other room, and she's talking plenty. I wish I could tell you what she's saying, but I can't. Maybe you can figure it out for yourself. You were the only ones there. I'm sure that you can imagine what she's telling."

Martinez leaves, hoping that the seeds planted will take root.

The room seems hotter, the lights brighter, the silence more oppressive; yet Denise's body language does not portray a woman in panic mode.

After fifteen minutes, a uniformed policeman comes in and puts a glass of water on the table in front of her. He leaves without comment.

Fifteen minutes after that, Colonel Mark Silverstine enters. He is accompanied by the female M.P., Lieutenant Stephanie Carlson. With them is another soldier carrying a court reporter's stenographic machine.

Silverstine sits down opposite Rakes. "All right, Denise. You know why we're here. I can't tell you what Evelyn Davis has told us in her statement."

He gestures toward the stenographer. "But you can figure that out for yourself. She may be your boyfriend or girlfriend or whatever you people call each other, but she doesn't want to die. She really doesn't want to die."

"There's something we can do for you. We have reason to believe that Evelyn isn't telling us everything that happened that night. She's holding something back, probably to protect herself. But you don't have to do that. And here's why: You don't have to go down for this. As of right now, you can get off the hook."

Denise looks directly at Silverstine for the first time.

"I'm authorized by the United States District Attorney and the Judge Advocate General at White Sands to offer you immunity from prosecution if you agree to cooperate in the prosecution of Evelyn Davis for murder."

"What does that mean?" Denise asks. Her voice is skeptical.

"Just what I said," Silverstine replied. "You help us see that justice is done in this case, and the Army won't give you any trouble about whatever part you played in it. I can't tell you what will happen with the lesbian thing; you know the rules about that. But that's the least of your worries when you're looking at a murder rap. You don't have to face that if you don't want to. And that's not just a promise. We'll put it in writing"

An anxious Denise Rakes asks, "Does Evelyn know you're doing this?"

"Don't you worry about what Evelyn knows or doesn't know. That's her problem. Your problem is deciding whether you want to be charged with first-degree murder and stay here in jail, or whether you want to go home now."

Denise looks Silverstine in the eye for a full minute.

"Tell me what I have to do."

EL PASO, TEXAS
19 APRIL 1983

With the exception of the visit from Martinez three hours before, Evelyn Davis has been alone in Interrogation Room B. The voices inside her head are stopped momentarily by a uniformed policewoman entering the room.

"Come on, honey. Time for a little change of scene." She handcuffs Evelyn and tries to lead her into the hallway.

"I'm not going anywhere till you tell me where my friend is: Denise, the other girl they brought in with me? What is happening to her?" Her voice is both agitated and defiant.

When the policewoman doesn't immediately respond, Evelyn pleads, "Please tell me something. Please, anything!"

"Well." the guard says, "far as I know, she's home. We let her go about half an hour ago. Why, didn't anybody tell you?"

"No! Nobody told me anything. I've just been sitting in there waiting."

Slowly, a shocked Evelyn walks with the policewoman to the front desk where two armed M.P.s are waiting. They take off the El Paso P.D. cuffs, manacle Evelyn with their own, and then lead her outside to a waiting Army cruiser.

That night as she lies on a wood bunk in a holding cell at the Fort Bliss M.P. station, she cannot understand why no one spent a great deal of time questioning her at the police station, why Denise has been released and she hasn't, and why is she still in custody when she isn't charged with any crime?

FORT BLISS, TEXAS
20 APRIL 1983

When Silverstine enters her cell, Evelyn stands at attention.

"You may be at ease. Specialist Davis, my name is Mark Silverstone, and I'm the provost marshal at White

Sands. I have here a warrant for your arrest on suspicion of the murder of Specialist Angela Kinney."

"The warrant is a formality because you're already in custody. But the legal process demands it. Now, have you been advised of your rights in this matter?"

Evelyn shakes her head. "I don't know. I think somebody talked to me about being quiet and getting a lawyer, but I can't remember."

"In that case we'll make sure." Silverstine takes out a card and reads Evelyn her Miranda rights.

"Do you understand them?"

"Yes sir."

"I also have a document from the United States district attorney charging you with first-degree murder in Angela Kinney's death and with being an accessory to first-degree murder. You are entitled to have a copy of these documents, or you may request that they be turned over to your attorney, should you obtain one."

Again Evelyn shakes her head. "I don't have a lawyer, but I suppose I'll have to get one. Save it for him."

"All right," Silverstine says. "The Judge Advocate General's office will appoint a military attorney to represent you for now. If you wish to hire a civilian attorney, that will be permissible. But an Army lawyer will act as your defense attorney temporarily and, if you want, permanently. Is that acceptable?"

Evelyn shrugs. "I guess so."

"Now," Silverstine continues, "this is what happens next. Sometime today you'll meet here with your appointed attorney to prepare for your arraignment. You know what an arraignment is?"

"No sir. I might, but I'm not sure."

"Probably tomorrow, you'll be taken before a US magistrate in El Paso: he's like a judge. You'll be formally charged with the murder of Angela Kinney. Your lawyer will be there. You'll enter a plea, guilty, not guilty, or no contest. And that will be about it. Unless the magistrate has other ideas, you'll be returned here for a short time, and then transferred to the stockade at Fort Sill in Oklahoma. We really don't have facilities for maximum-security prisoners."

Evelyn nods without looking at Silverstine.

"Evelyn," he said now in a softer tone. "Do you understand what's going on here?"

"Yes sir. I know Angela's dead. I know you all think I did it. I didn't do it; but I guess it won't do no good to tell anybody that now."

Silverstine shrugs. "You had a chance to tell us more when you were at the El Paso police station, but you didn't want to. Anyway, you'll have an opportunity to tell your side of it at the trial. If you plead not guilty, there'll be a court-martial. You'll have a good lawyer and the chance to call witnesses and produce evidence for your defense. That's about all I can tell you now. Anything else?"

Evelyn looks up at Silverstine for the first time. "Yes, there is. Can you tell me what has happened to Denise Rakes, and what will happen to her now?"

"All I can tell you is that she was questioned about Kinney's death. She has agreed to tell us what she knows about it and to be a witness in your prosecution. She's been let go, and as far as I know she's returned to whatever she does."

"Is she going to be in any trouble?"

"I can't answer that. It hasn't all been worked out yet. Why? Are you worried about her?"

Evelyn stares at the cell wall. "You could say that. Yeah, I'm worried about her, but. I don't think you'd understand. What about my kids?"

Silverstine, who had gotten up replies, "Don't worry. I promise that your two boys will be well taken care of."

The M.P. unlocks the cell door. As Silverstine walks towards the corridor, he turns back to Evelyn "If I were you, I'd be more worried about yourself."

At about one o'clock that afternoon, an M.P. leads Evelyn into a sparsely furnished unused office in the M.P. station. An Army captain sits behind a dust covered desk on which rests a single file folder.

"You may sit down, Specialist," the officer says. Turning to the M.P., "You can wait outside. This will be a privileged discussion between attorney and client. I don't need any protection."

Evelyn sits in the wooden chair in front of the desk.

"My name is Captain Leroy Howard. I have been appointed your defense counsel, at least through the arraignment tomorrow. I am assuming you are going to plead innocent. Is that correct?"

Evelyn nods. "I didn't kill Angela."

Howard purses his lips. "Then that's how you'll plead."

Never having dealt with an attorney before, Evelyn thinks that if she has to have one, Howard looks to be a good choice. He's black and powerfully built. His starched khakis, brightly polished brass and general air of command impress her.

He stares hard at Evelyn and then clears his throat. "Let's get something straight before we start, Specialist Davis. They appointed me to defend you; they didn't assign me to be your friend or tell me I had to approve of who and what you are. As a matter of fact, I don't approve of who and what you are. As a black man, I don't appreciate people like you and your homo-lovers making it harder for the rest of us to hold our heads up. The Army is one of the most integrated institutions in society. It doesn't help the situation when people like you foul up and make the rest of us have to stand up for you. Understand?"

Evelyn doesn't understand. She has never thought that race and sexual preference ought to make that much difference.

"Do you understand?" repeats Captain Howard in a loud voice

Inwardly stunned, she merely answers, "Yes sir."

Howard opens her file. "We need to get a few things straight here. The name on your 201 file is Evelyn Davis. Is Davis your original name or a married name?"

"Married, sir. My maiden name is Evelyn Riley. My husband was Tony Davis, a sergeant. We're divorced now, and I think he's stationed overseas somewhere."

"All right. It says you have two children. Are they Davis's?"

"One is: the younger one. The first one's father was named Simpson. We were just together a little while, and he split."

"What happened between you and this Sergeant Davis? Why the divorce?"

Evelyn gazes out the window for a few seconds before answering. "Sir, this might be hard to explain."

"Go ahead. We don't want any nasty surprises later on."

"Simpson was an accident. I didn't really like having regular sex with men, but he came along before I enlisted. He got me pregnant. I almost lost the baby. He was premature and had to spend six months in the hospital before I could bring him home."

Howard continues methodically. "And you kept the baby and stayed at home with whom, your parents?"

"Just my mother and my brothers."

"When did this Davis come along?"

"I met him in the Army."

"Did he know you were gay?"

"He knew about that up front. But we liked each other. He was fun, a sweet guy, a great dancer and liked to have a good time"

"If you just liked each other, how come you got married and had his baby?"

"I wanted another child, maybe because I almost lost the first one. Just because I feel more like a man than a woman, that didn't mean I didn't want to be a mother, or at least a parent with children of my own."

Howard makes another face. "That doesn't sound like much of a basis for a marriage."

"It was enough for Tony and me. I wanted a male who'd give me a baby, and Tony was good for that."

"If he was so great and everything was so hunky-dory, why'd you split up?"

"We both knew we weren't a real man and wife. I didn't need him. The baby came. It wasn't part of his deal, so we got divorced."

"So you kept this baby, even without a father."

"Yes sir. I'm happy I did."

"Where are these children now? Are they still with you?"

Evelyn nods affirmatively. "They live with me at White Sands in my quarters there."

"I mean where they are right now, today? Do you know?"

"I don't know. When the M.P.s picked me up, they said they'd be sure somebody would take care of them."

Howard makes a note on the cover of the file. "We'll check into it and make sure that they are in good hands. One more thing before we're finished. It says in your file that sometimes you call yourself, Bandit Riley. Where does that come from?"

Evelyn shrugs. "Well, Riley is my maiden name. And I just kind of liked the sound of Bandit. That's where it comes from."

Howard stands, file in hand. "We'll stay with Evelyn Davis, if you don't mind. I don't think any court is going to look kindly on somebody named Bandit."

He calls for the guard, and then has a final word for Evelyn. "The Army and the justice system say you're entitled to the best defense. I don't think I can deliver that. My heart and soul aren't in it. I'll see you through the arraignment tomorrow and make sure you get all the rights you're entitled to. But after that, I think you'd either better get a civilian attorney, or have the JAG appoint somebody else."

All Evelyn can again say, is, "Yes sir."

EL PASO, TEXAS
21 APRIL 1983

Captain Howard is waiting in the courtroom in the EI Paso federal building when two uniformed MPs lead Evelyn Davis in through a back door near the judge's bench.

"Take the cuffs off," Howard motions to Evelyn to sit with him at the counsel table.

The magistrate is already seated. The only other people in the room are a court reporter, an assistant U.S. district attorney standing by the bench, and, seated in the spectators' area, Detective Sergeant Ray Martinez of the EI Paso police.

"The United States vs. Evelyn Davis." The magistrate asks Evelyn and her attorney to stand. The magistrate continues: "Let the record show that the government is represented in the person of Mr. Richard Sanders of the U.S. Attorney's Office and that the defendant is present in court, accompanied by counsel"

He opens the file in front of him. "This case is brought by complaints lodged against the defendant by the U.S. government, charging murder in the first degree and being an accessory after the fact to first-degree murder. This proceeding is for the purpose of allowing the defendant to hear the charges against her and to enter her plea thereto."

The magistrate makes a "come here" gesture to Evelyn and Captain Howard.

Addressing them both, he asks, "Have these charges been presented to the defendant, does she understand the nature of them, and has she been advised of her constitutional rights?"

Howard nudges Evelyn. "Yes sir," she answers.

"Do you wish to claim the right to have the charges read to you at this time?"

"No sir. I know what they are."

The magistrate turns to Sanders. "Anything from the government?"

"No, Your Honor. We're ready to proceed with the arraignment."

"Very well." In adopting a more formal tone, the magistrate raises his voice.

"Specialist Evelyn Davis, you have heard the charges brought against you and affirm that you understand them. Are you now prepared to enter a plea?"

"Yes sir."

"To the charge of murder in the first-degree, what is your plea?"

"Not guilty."

"To the charge of accessory to murder in the first degree, what is your plea?"

"Not guilty."

"Pleas having been entered, the defendant is ordered remanded into custody. As I'm sure the parties realize, no request for bail on these charges can be considered."

He closes the file. "Are we to set a date for a preliminary hearing or leave that open for determination by the military court?"

"Your Honor," Howard says, speaking for the first and last time, "the defendant has indicated that she desires to waive preliminary hearing."

The magistrate nods. "Very well. The record will reflect that. Is there anything else before this court at this time?"

He pauses. "Then, this proceeding is concluded."

Gathering his papers, the judge leaves the courtroom.

Howard nods to the M.P. who puts the handcuffs back on Evelyn and lead her away. She looks back at Howard, as if looking for a word or sign-anything, but he is talking with the federal prosecutor.

"I guess we're all done," Howard says. "The JAG will take it from here on our side, and she'll have a new lawyer as soon as I can sign off and get someone else appointed."

"What's the matter?" Sanders asks. "Case too tough for you?"

"You might say something like that."

Alone in the back of the courtroom, Ray Martinez slowly gets up and heads for the exit.

WHITE SANDS MISSILE RANGE
25 APRIL 1983

That Patrick J. Bailey would end up in the Army was a foregone conclusion. When the male members of his family bled, it was drab olive. His grandfather had been a career officer. His father drove one of George Patton's tanks through France and into Germany. When the Bailey boys graduated from high school, they enlisted. Period!

Young Pat deviated somewhat from the family tradition: When he graduated from high school, he went to a junior college, the same one his mother had attended. He stayed long enough to win a scholarship to the University of California-Berkeley, and delayed his entry into the Army until he graduated from Berkeley and then from the University's Hasting College of Law.

From boyhood, he had had only one career dream/fantasy: to be a criminal defense attorney. While other kids dreamt of being firemen or cowboys, Patrick saw himself as the new Clarence Darrow. The law was for him his avocation, not his vocation.

The next piece of his personal jigsaw puzzle fell into place when Patrick J. Bailey, J.D., newly commissioned as a captain, was assigned to the U.S. Army Trial Defense Service, a separate command within the Judge Advocate General Corps.

Officers assigned to Trial Defense respond only to Washington, and are only nominally under the command and jurisdiction of local Army authorities.

This arm's-length relationship is designed to give the Army's defense lawyers a degree of independence that insulates them from command pressures that could compromise their positions as advocates for the accused.

WHITE SANDS MISSILE RANGE 26 APRIL 1983

Evelyn Davis doesn't know what to expect from her new defense attorney appointed by the Army. Her experience with Captain Howard has her anticipating the worst: another superior officer looking down on her as a soldier and as a person: probably a straight white male who'd let his contempt for her lifestyle get in the way of her defense.

"Hi," her new lawyer says as Evelyn comes into the interview room in the M.P. station.

He stands up and offers his hand. "My name's Pat Bailey. It looks like we're going to be seeing a lot of each other."

She takes his hand hesitantly and mumbles something that ends in "Sir." To herself Evelyn thinks '*This white guy looks like Dennis-the-Menace with sun glasses and a small tuff of hair is sticking up on the top of his head.*

"Please sit down," Bailey says. "Let's get acquainted."

He folds his hands on the bare wooden table and leans forward. "So you're Evelyn Davis, my client."

She just nods, but inwardly says to herself, *"Is this guy serous?"*

Bailey isn't surprised by his reception. In his defense of other military suspects, he has come to expect hostility, sullenness, silence and non-cooperation. Besides, he knows what went on between Specialist Davis and Captain Howard, and figures that he has some overcoming to do.

Evelyn sits slumped in her chair, avoiding Bailey's eyes.

"They tell me you call yourself Bandit sometimes," Bailey said. "Where did that come from?"

She shrugs. "I don't know. Like I told that other captain, it just kind of happened. I like the sound of it better than a girl's name. Bandit kind of fits the way I've live."

"Would you rather I call you Bandit or Evelyn?"

"I don't care."

"Well, I have to call you something, and to tell the truth I don't care either. Sometimes I might call you Bandit, sometimes Evelyn. But in court, we'd probably better stick with Evelyn. Okay?"

"Yeah, I guess."

Bailey continues. "Now, while we're on that subject, let's get the pronouns straightened out. The he-or-she business: most of the rest of the world is going to call you she or her. What do you call yourself?"

The answer literally explodes with such emphasis as to catch Bailey by surprise. "A man!"

"Good enough for me," Bailey answers. He hides his surprise well. "You know yourself better than anybody else does. You can pick what you want to be; but for the trial and all the outside stuff, we're probably on safer ground if we stick with she and her. That may not be real comfortable for you, but at this point, it's the least of our worries."

He leans back in his chair and crosses his legs. "Have they told you how long you'll be here?"

"They said in court they'd keep me here for a while and then transfer me to Fort Sill."

"Well, that's a long way off. But I can get up there as often as I need to, and while you're still here, we can at least get a good start on building you a defense."

Evelyn shakes her head skeptically. "I don't know about that. It's only me against what Denise says. They believe her. If they didn't, she'd be here with me."

Bailey laughs. "Yeah, it sounds like an open-and-shut case. But that works two ways. The Army thinks Rakes has it all wrapped up for them, but the trouble is that's all they've got. So it comes down to you versus her. No! You and I versus her.

Bailey hopes that, maybe, she will cooperate in her own defense after that statement, but her body language says no. She has held back on Captain Howard and everyone else she'd been in contact with.

He takes a yellow legal pad and ballpoint pen out of a worn leather briefcase. "So let's start organizing this deal. Why don't you just tell me in your own words what happened the night that Angela Kinney died?"

Evelyn hadn't expected to cut to the chase that quickly. She turns away from Bailey who senses her desire to force closure on the meeting.

El Paso
30 Apri1 1983

Detective Ray Martinez spots the man he is looking for sitting in a back booth at Roberto's Inferno, one of the city's less upscale nightclubs. He is easy to pick out. In his power suit, power shirt, and power tie, he couldn't have looked more out of place. He clearly belongs in establishments with hanging ferns and polished brass railings.

Martinez, on the other hand, fits right in. The Inferno seems an appropriate place for the solidly built detective dressed in a suit that no one would mistake as coming from Brooks Brothers.

Martinez slides into the booth and sticks a hand across the table.

"Glad you could make it. I wasn't sure whether I asked you to bite off more than you could chew."

"No problem, pal," Joel Cohen replies. "I'll stretch a little any time for my favorite cop."

In his out of fashion suit and cheap haircut, Martinez looks more like a cop than a cop should look. Anyone noticing the contrast between him and Cohen would wonder what in the world brought this unlikely pair together.

It's simple. Cohen owed Martinez, big-time. One of the attorney's early clients would still be in jail if Martinez's penchant for even-handed, tenacious investigating hadn't turned up more evidence for the defense than it did for the prosecution. Since that time, Cohen has built up a lucrative criminal defense practice and with it an expanding waistline. The two have stayed in touch and become friends: at least to the extent that a cop and a defense lawyer can.

They exchange pleasantries, catching up on each other's lives since the last time they met. Then Cohen says, "Okay. Let's get to it. You asked me to dig up what I could find about an Army captain, Patrick Bailey, at White Sands. The answer is that there isn't much."

"I didn't think there would be," Martinez answers. "But I'm not looking for any dirt on the guy. What I need to know is what kind of man he is. Is he a straight shooter or not"

"That I can answer," Cohen says. "From what I hear from guys in the local bar and around the base, he's bright as hell, but hasn't let it go to his head. Plays the chameleon: keeps his smarts to himself. Plays it low key. By the time you figure it out, he's gotcha."

Cohen gestures to the bartender to bring another round. "Bailey's sort of a star in the Army legal outfits. He's the guy they give the tough ones to. As far as anybody knows, he doesn't lose many."

"Spit-and-polish military? By the book?"

Cohen laughs so hard, he almost spills his drink. "Not hardly. He knows how to play the Army game, but when the chips are down, he goes his own way. Let me give you an example: In the building where his office is located, the regulations state that you can't hang anything on the walls that doesn't have a frame around it. Kind of chicken shit, but that's the way it is. Anyway, a guy who works there tells me that Bailey's office is wallpapered, with pictures of Miss Piggy and a bunch of other stuff that drove the brass crazy. Not a picture frame in sight."

Martinez nods in approval. "Sounds like the kind of guy to go with. Tell me this; if you gave him a loaded gun, something that might turn a case around, would he use it?"

Cohen replies. "Definitely. He's not only a straight shooter; he's a sharpshooter."

"That's basically what I wanted to know," Martinez said.

"Why? You involved in a case with him?"

"Not exactly. My part of it is pretty much finished. His is only beginning. He's the attorney for a soldier on trial for murder-one. I have a firecracker that I'm thinking of giving to Bailey. It might not help, but it sure wouldn't hurt."

"Well," Cohen said, "it sounds like something's going on here that I probably don't need or want to know about, so let's call it a night. Drinks are on me."

WHITE SANDS MISSILE RANGE
30 APRIl 1983

Shortly after breakfast, a female M.P. appears at Evelyn's cell door, carrying an armful of clothing.

"Here. Put these on, Looks like you're going on a little road trip."

"Fort Sill? I didn't think they were taking me there yet."

"I don't know, babe. The man said that I get dressed up and take you out to the front desk. Better get with it."

Evelyn takes off her fatigues with the "P" stenciled on the back and sorts through the clothing the M.P. has brought. She finds a heavily starched, neatly pressed camouflage utility uniform, complete with underwear, socks, a matching cap and highly shined combat boots. On the sleeve is the badge of her rank, Specialist Four, but there is no name tape above the breast pocket.

Evelyn hurriedly dons the uniform, making sure the gig line is straight and the pant legs properly bloused over the boot tops.

"Let's go," the guard says.

They go down the hall to the front desk area, where Evelyn is surprised to see Captain Patrick Bailey waiting.

"Morning. You look sharp today-very military. Come. We're going for a ride."

He leads the way out of the station to his car, a battered old Volvo wagon. They get in and drive off.

Anticipating Evelyn's questions, Bailey explains that under the Uniform Code of Military Justice, an accused is entitled to reasonable measures in assisting in the preparation of his defense. Bailey had applied to the Judge Advocate General's Office to have Evelyn released in his custody for the day. Surprisingly, the application had been endorsed by Colonel Mark Silverstine.

"For the record, we're going out to see where Angela's body was found. I need you to show me some things

and answer some questions before you go off to Sill. Off
the record, we're doing no such thing. I just figure that
you needed a break from that cell. Besides, it'll give us
a chance to just visit about some stuff without being all
formal and lawyerly about it."

"You mean," Evelyn asks, "they trust me to just go off
with you alone and not try to escape or anything?"

Bailey chuckles and pats the 45 caliber automatic
holstered at his right hip. "They checked this out to me
yesterday. If you try anything, I'm authorized to shoot
you." Laughing, he adds, "You'd better not try anything,
because I don't even know how to load one of these
things."

They drive south from the missile range to El Paso,
where Bailey pulls into a Burger King and parks.

"Let's have coffee."

When they have their coffee and are seated in a
booth, Bailey explains to Evelyn how the court-martial
will work.

"Forget about what you've seen on TV. There won't
necessarily be 12 people on the jury. We'll start out with
about that many, but both the prosecutor and I will be
able to get rid of jurors we don't like for one reason or
another. We could end up with as few as five or six.

He explains that the jurors would all be Army
officers of differing ranks, mostly male, mostly white.
The judge would be a high-ranking officer assigned by
the Judge Advocate General Corps, and the prosecutor
an experienced attorney also from the JAG.

"There's another big difference from civilian trials.
The jury doesn't have to reach a unanimous verdict. It
just takes a majority vote to convict."

He injects what he hopes is a reassuring note. "You're still protected by the assumption of innocence. That is, the jury is supposed to start out thinking you're innocent unless the Army can prove you're guilty. You don't have to prove anything. You have to be found guilty beyond a reasonable doubt. That's hard to explain, but what it means is that the Army really has to nail down its case."

Evelyn has listened quietly, nodding and sipping coffee. "Can you tell me something?" she asks.

"Sure, if I can."

"They're charging me with two things—murder and accessory. Where does that come from?"

Bailey looks away for a moment. The question comes close to getting at one of the things that bothers him most about the case.

"That comes from the government wanting to get a conviction, one way or the other. If the jury thinks you strangled Angela Kinney, they'll convict you of murder. If they think Denise Rakes strangled her and you helped or even just stood there and didn't do anything, they'll convict you as an accessory. Right now, they are betting that you killed Angela."

Evelyn shakes her head. "I have to take my medicine for what I did, but if they can put two charges on me, what about her? Isn't Denise charged with anything?"

"Somebody did a "pick-and-choose": probably because Denise didn't shoot her husband and you did."

Not waiting for a response, Bailey quickly changes the subject. "By virtue of their indoctrination in the Army and their own personal views, the people on the jury most likely will have little or no tolerance for gays and presumably lesbians in the military. That's one big problem. Here's another."

"Denise Rakes is a visually attractive female. Through her activities as a bartender at the Officers' Club and assistant cashier at the base branch bank, she will be known to some of the jurors."

A picture of Rakes has already been formed in Bailey's mind: married, beautiful, charming, possibly college educated. He can easily understand why, beyond the shooting, the military has focused on Davis. He knows the contrast between his client and Rakes is significant.

He continues. "Rakes isn't charged with anything because the government promised her immunity from prosecution if she testified against you. You can think that either she sold you out or that the Army is willing to do anything to get a nice, neat conviction as soon as possible. Either one or both may be right."

Bailey sips at his coffee and clears his throat. "If the jury has trouble tolerating and understanding you, I'll try to change that. To do that, I need you to educate me. So walk me through the various roles in the gay-lesbian community. Can you do that?"

"Both?" Evelyn asks.

"Both."

The words flow as if they have been long waiting an invitation.

"Okay. First, there are gays: men who look like men and usually act like men but are sexually focused on other men. Then you have the occasional transvestites who get it on by dressing and acting out like women. Drag queens are sort of the same, but they do their thing up front and in the open, well sort of."

"With women, you have what you would term lesbians: women who look like women and act like women, but engage in same-sex intercourse."

Bailey is privately surprised and encouraged by the way Evelyn can articulate a complicated subject. *'Maybe she'll be pretty good on the stand after all.'* "Take me through some definitions: one at a time. I want to make notes."

"All right," she replies. "Dykes: women who look female but act male - Fems: women who look and act female but are attracted to females -Butches: women who look and act like males. - Bisexuals: that's just AC/DC."

"And you?" Bailey asks.

Evelyn looks away and doesn't reply for so long that Bailey again anticipates a premature closure when the silence is shattered by a voice that resonates with anger.

With her hands upright and apart on the table, she stares at the space between them, Evelyn states, "I'm a freak-a fucking freak: a man in a woman's body. I've been trapped there all my life. Until Denise, no one could accept me. I could not accept me!"

Bailey knows that what he just heard, if repeated in a courtroom, would strain the bounds of credibility too far. On the pad, he writes a note to check her mental health records. Sensing the need to change the subject, but in a meaningful way, he leans across the table.

"You've seemed awfully anxious to protect Denise," he said. "I get the sense that you're not protesting your innocence as strongly as most people would in your situation. You think you might change your mind about that if you thought about what she's doing to you?"

Evelyn looks away. This conversation has gone too far for her.

Both realize that today's excursion wraps up the bulk of their pre-trial communications. It is Bailey's last opportunity for a meeting before Evelyn is taken to Fort Sill.

As they get ready to leave, Bailey says, "One more thing. You're not facing this all alone. We'll have witnesses that can knock down some of what Denise Rakes is gonna say."

They pull up in front of the M.P. station. Bailey gets out and makes a show of escorting Evelyn to the front desk, as if she were a dangerous prisoner and he's keeping a wary eye on her.

"I don't know if I'll see you again before the court-martial," he says, "but if anything comes up I'll let you know, and you do the same. Just let the people at Sill know that you need to see your attorney."

As Evelyn gets out of the car, it dawns on her she hadn't the slightest idea of what, if anything, her attorney is planning.

Bailey drives away thinking that, except for a few odds and ends and interviewing minor witnesses, he is as prepared as he can be to offer a defense for Evelyn. He doesn't know that an important piece of the jigsaw puzzle that is Evelyn Riley's life is yet to fall into place.

El Paso Police Department
30 April 1983

Unannounced, Colonel Mark Silverstine walks into Ray Martinez's office. This time, it is Martinez's turn to offer a cup of coffee.

Caught a bit off guard, the detective addresses Silverstine by his first name. "Mark, I don't like the case."

Before the colonel could reply, Martinez continues. "I think a serious mistake is being made," He pushes a folder across the desk to Silverstine.

Silverstine quickly examines the papers in the folder. Then with emphasis, he shoves the folder back at Martinez. With a few more inches, it would have been floor-bound.

"Is that what you called me here to show me? Well, let me explain it to you. The U. S. Army needs this case to disappear, and that's just what is going to happen. This is not a perfect world. Sometimes there is going to be collateral damage. What is done is in the interest of the big picture, and you seemingly have a chronic problem with the big picture. That's probably why you have been passed over twice for the top job. Let it go! Do I make myself clear'?"

"Sky-blue," Martinez responds.

Without any further words, Silverstine gets up and leaves. The closed door quivers for a few extra seconds.

WHITE SANDS MISSILE RANGE
30 APRIL 1983

That night, after delivering Evelyn back to the M.P.s and checking in at his office, Pat Bailey stops at a local supermarket to pick up something for dinner.

He has not noticed the dark blue sedan which has followed his car from the front gate of the post.

Bailey makes a few purchases at the store and returns to his car. He's surprised to find the car doors locked. Figuring that the car is so old and disreputable that no self-respecting thief would give it a second glance, he seldom bothers to lock its doors.

Unlocking the driver's side door, he perceives a large manila envelope on the front seat. His name is scrawled across the front of it.

Putting his grocery bag on the car's hood, Bailey opens the envelope. A second envelope falls out.

On it is printed: St. Joseph Hospital, Omaha, Nebraska. The envelope bears in large red letters the words: **'CONFIDENTIAL FILE'**

FORT SILL, OKLAHOMA
21 MAY 1983

Evelyn's experience in jail at White Sands Missile Range has not prepared her for what she encounters at Fort Sill.

At the missile range M.P. station, she was kept in what amounted to a temporary holding cell. The only other prisoners were minor offenders who came and went, usually for a day or two at a time, and they were held in a separate facility down a hallway from Evelyn's cell. Her only contacts were the M.P.s, mostly females, who brought her meals and mail and looked in on her from time to time.

The stockade at Sill is different. It houses prisoners from Army posts throughout the Southwest. Its inmate population is nearly as large as some civilian penitentiaries. Most of these inmates have already been convicted in courts-martial and are serving their sentences. The Army believes more in incarceration than rehabilitation. The majority of the prisoners have been sent to Sill on drug-related charges, but there is a liberal sprinkling of violent offenders.

The prison's population is entirely male. Because she is the only woman prisoner, Evelyn is housed in a dormitory-style room which previously had confined twenty men. She is not allowed in the exercise yard when male prisoners are there. She can't go to the exercise room or the day room unless no other inmates are there, which is seldom. In the mess hail, she sits at a separate table and is not allowed to talk to other prisoners.

However, the restriction applies only one way: The male prisoners can and do talk to her. "Hey, baby, you wanta try some of this?" - "You come over here and I'll show you what you been missing." - "You ain't bad-lookin' for a queer." - "I didn't know dykes liked killing each other."

Evelyn takes as much of this as she can. Her tray spills on the table as she jumps up. "You bastards! There's two things I like to do, and one of 'em is kick ass! Anybody wants some, come over here!"

After this outbreak, Evelyn is restricted to her room. Meals are brought to her. She is not allowed to lie on her bed during daylight hours. Her choice is to pace her cell or sit on the hard wooden chair that is bolted to the floor.

She receives almost daily letters from Cecilia Riley and an occasional encouraging note from Pat Bailey. Otherwise, she is completely out of touch with the outside world. Bailey had offered the theory that the Army transferred her to Fort Sill, not because White Sands didn't have the facilities for her, but to keep her under wraps, far from Fort Bliss and even farther from the inquiring presence of the media.

She fills the vacant hours with musings on how she has arrived at her present state and with worry and regrets over what has gone wrong with her relationship with Denise.

These are accompanied by other thoughts: *'If this is what I have to do, I can do it.! I'm tired of wondering whether I'm going to die. I'm going to die!'*

Fort Sill, Oklahoma
28 June 1983

Evelyn's period of what amounted to solitary confinement finally comes to an end, or at least, to a more humane modification. She is moved out of the twenty bed dormitory room into a twelve-by- twelve foot cell in an unused, isolated block of the stockade which formerly had been a quarantine area for prisoners with infectious diseases. It has the standard metal bunk, metal table and chair, and stainless steel bathroom fixtures, and in that respect is no different from any other cell in any other prison. But to Evelyn, it is luxurious, compared with the echoing hollow box in which she had been confined. Her new cell has a shower stall in one corner and even a small window, high on the outside wall, through which she can see clouds by day and stars by night.

Her court-martial being tentatively scheduled for late September or early October at White Sands, the stockade commander had been prodded to the conclusion that given the length of time his prisoner is to be at Fort Sill, it might be considered cruel and unusual punishment for her to remain locked away from virtually all human contact. It was pointed out that more dangerous and violent inmates enjoy relatively 'normal' terms of incarceration. The prodding had been provided by Captain Patrick Bailey. On one of his visits to Fort

Sill, he had a brief conversation with the C .O. in which he mentioned such terms as 'inspector general,' 'habeas corpus', bad publicity in the media, racial and gender discrimination, and congressional interest. Disliking hassles as much as anyone in uniform, the commander decided that prudence was the better part of prison discipline.

Now Evelyn can visit the exercise yard accompanied by a woman M.P. when no male prisoners are there. Occasionally she is taken to the mess hall under the same arrangements, and no longer has to take all her meals alone in her cell. The M.P.s arrange for her to work out in the weight room during times it isn't in use.

Even this special regimen doesn't protect Evelyn from the unwanted attention of the men in the stockade. As she passes to and from her limited activities, she is still subjected to the catcalls and obscenities. But she knows that as much as the other prisoners may despise what she stands for, they can't get at her.

On this day late in June, she has another visit from Bailey. The M.P. unlocks the cell door to let Patrick Bailey in. He is carrying a large cardboard box. "Here, a little gift from the outside to help you pass the time of day."

Evelyn opens the box and finds a combination AM-FM radio and audio cassette player, complete with headphones. Tucked into a corner of the box are two tapes, 'The Key to Life' by Stevie Wonder and 'Tug of War' by Paul McCartney.

"This is great," says a really excited Evelyn Davis. "But I don't think we're supposed to have stuff like this in here."

Bailey shakes his head. "You can if your lawyer makes enough waves — and if he gets an authorization endorsed by the head M.P. at White Sands. They still have some jurisdiction over you. Colonel Silverstine thought his authority included tape players. And by the way, you'll be getting a typewriter one of these days. I told 'em it's important for you to have one to assist in the preparation of your defense, and they bought into it. You can write letters and poetry or whatever."

The voices in her head and Evelyn are both silent. She can't think of anything to say.

In this same visit, Bailey gingerly explores further the sexual aspects of her case, to further satisfy himself that he understands his client's background.

"Evelyn, you've told me you feel like you're a man trapped in a woman's body. I think I have some idea what you mean by that, and we need to talk about it in terms of your trial."

Evelyn nods. She thought she and Bailey had covered all the ground they needed to in advance of the court-martial, but if he wants to talk some more, she is ready. She doesn't have anything else to do. "As I understand it," Bailey said, "people with some kind of mixed or confused sexuality can develop a very strong anger toward life in general. You feel any of that?"

Evelyn thinks a moment. "Yeah, I guess so. I've always had a pretty hot temper, and I know I've always felt like I got a raw deal as far as sex and things are concerned. Okay, you can say that. Yes, I'm a pretty angry person, most of the time!"

"Now this gets pretty touchy, Evelyn. The Army is treating this like a crime of passion, but still premeditated

52

murder. They're gonna say you killed Angela Kinney as the result of jealousy, in a lesbian love triangle."

"I know that," Evelyn replies.

"But you and I are going on the basis that there really weren't three women involved in this — you and Rakes and Angela. There were two women and a man — the man being you. Isn't that the way you see it?"

Evelyn's thoughts come back to her: *'I am the man. Denise is definitely the woman. That's the way it is for me. But I don't think anybody would understand that or believe it.'* She answers simply "Yes".

"I hate to say this, but if you are convicted of murder, we may be able to use this perspective to get you a lighter sentence."

"You mean a lighter sentence than death?"

"Yeah, that's what I mean," Bailey replies.

Omaha, Nebraska
20 June 1978

In her mid-sixties, Cecilia Riley is a plump, sixtyish woman with long silver-gray hair.

Cecilia Riley's life has turned a corner. Since enrolling in the New Careers program, she has risen determinedly to the challenge of getting a college education while working at a job helping children and caring for her own brood.

It has been hard. But then, her life has always been hard. And now she is closing in on a goal which a few short years ago seemed an unattainable fantasy. A few weeks ago, she completed the last of her course work for her degree. In anticipation, she has applied for teaching positions in public and private Omaha school systems.

Tonight, as she hurries toward a women's meeting at the Church of the Living God, Cecilia mentally gives thanks for the opportunities bestowed on her while at the same time praying for guidance as to what, if anything, she can do for her daughter, Evelyn.

As she nears the church, she notices an unusually large number of cars parked along the street and guesses that something besides the women's circle meeting must be taking place. She goes in a side door and down the stairs to the social hall. She opens the door and stops abruptly.

Gathered in the hall is nearly the entire congregation of the Church of the Living God, Cecilia's family, and a representation of the surrounding neighborhood.

A huge banner is strung across the front of the room: CONGRATULATIONS, CECILIA.

The room is festooned with balloons and streamers. An enormous cake forms the center piece of a food-laden table. Written on it, in blue icing, are the words BACHELOR'S DEGREE and NEW CAREER.

The room breaks into a cheer as Cecilia stands stock-still in surprise. When the happy tumult dies down, the regional director of Cecilia's program steps forward. He welcomes the crowd, and then recites a list of Cecilia's accomplishments that include valedictorian of her class (first in the nation in the New Careers enterprise).

The director of New Careers then introduces a man who had been standing quietly at the back of the hall. James Farmer, Secretary of the U.S. Health and Human Services Department. He presents Cecilia with her certificate of graduation and announces her appointment to a teaching position at one of the magnet schools in the public system.

Further applause and cheers greet his recitation. He asks Cecilia to say a few words, but she is speechless. All she can do is step to the microphone and mumble her thanks to God for putting her where she is, to all who had helped her through the hard years, and to her family and friends for their encouragement. The tears suddenly come freely to a woman who has endured so much without weeping.

At home that night, after tidying the house, putting in a load of laundry and saying her prayers, Cecilia lays in bed wondering at her good fortune. She has emerged from the long, dark tunnel of poverty and abandonment, but not from fear. Her Evie is in harm's way.

***

WHITE SANDS MISSILE RANGE
14 SEPTEMBER 1983

When Bailey receives his official list of trial participants, he notes that the military judge had a familiar name — too familiar, as far as Evelyn's case is concerned.

The judge, a JAG colonel, had once lectured on military legal procedures in a class Bailey was taking in law school. Bailey remembered some of the things the lecturer had said, and realized that they could spell bad news for his client.

Five weeks before the court-martial is to convene, Bailey requests a private conference with the judge who had arrived at White Sands from his duty station at the Presidio in California.

In this meeting, Bailey reminds the judge of the lecture he had given at the law school, and that he, Bailey, had been in the class.

"Sir," Bailey said, "this is uncomfortable for me, but in the interests of my client, I have to say that some of the remarks you made that day indicate a degree of potential bias on your part."

The colonel appears to be taken aback and asks Bailey to elaborate.

Bailey said he recalls, and that it was in his class notes, that the colonel had expressed the opinion that gays had no place in the Army, and that the administration of military justice should be directed toward getting them out.

"I don't remember saying that, Captain," the judge answers.

Bailey states that he can validate his recollection, from his notes; and, if necessary, through affidavits from other lawyers who had been present in the classroom. "I don't think either of us, or the Army, would want to have to go through all that."

The colonel ponders that. Finally he says: "Captain, I assure you that whatever personal opinion I have about the presence and role of homosexuals in the Army, it wouldn't get in the way of my presiding fairly and impartially over this court. But, having said that, I also have to say that I recognize that justice not only must be administered fairly, it must be seen to be administered fairly."

Bailey detects victory.

"Therefore," the judge said, "we needn't pursue this formally. I voluntarily rescue myself from this case, and the JAG can appoint a new judge. That's okay with you?"

Bailey replies that that is what he had in mind. He apologizes to the colonel for the discomfort the conversation has caused, and excuses himself.

There is more than a touch of guile in Bailey's approach to this matter. He knows that even though there is no record of his talk with the colonel, White Sands is a comparatively small post. The military legal world is even a smaller community. Bailey figures that when it is learned that a full colonel had gotten burned over his attitude toward gays, the official conduct of others connected with the case may become a little more circumspect.

FORT SILL, OKLAHOMA
23 SEPTEMBER 1983

After his first couple of visits to Fort Sill, Captain Pat Bailey is allowed to consult with his client in her cell rather than in a visitation room. Today, as he sits on the edge of her bunk, he tells her it will be his last visit to the stockade.

Evelyn frowns. She has looked forward to their conversations. Bailey has become good company.

"Aren't I going to see you any more?" she asks.

"Sure. But not here. The day after tomorrow you're being transferred back to White Sands. The court-martial is set for October 18th, and you'll need to be handy for any last-minute stuff that comes up."

"I won't mind that." She tells Bailey that while her circumstances have improved at Sill, she still feels isolated and alone, more so than she had been in the prison at White Sands. "What more do we have to do to get ready?"

Bailey shakes his head. "Unless something comes up that we haven't been counting on, we're as ready as we can be. Next time I see you will be back at White Sands, and not long after that we'll be in court."

Evelyn is relieved. She feels that she is already serving her sentence. The transfer to White Sands will be a welcome change of scenery. She is both anxious and apprehensive to begin the process that will determine whether she lives or dies.

As he leaves, Patrick Bailey knows that despite the improvement in their relationship, there is still a wall behind which he is not permitted.

WHITE SANDS COURTROOM
18 OCTOBER 1983

The current apex of the criminal justice system at the White Sands Missile Range headquarters is a converted classroom, usually used for briefings and training courses. Full-blown courts-martial on capital charges are such a rarity at the relatively small post that the provision of a courtroom with all the trappings representing the majesty of the law would have been an extravagance.

At the court-martial of Specialist 4 Evelyn Davis, beginning at 1305 hours, the military judge will sit behind an ordinary office desk, placed on a dais constructed for the occasion, and backed by the United States and U.S. Army flags on standards.

The officers making up the jury will sit behind a folding table on another dais. The court reporter will sit at a small table in front of the judge's "bench," and the sergeant-at-arms

The bailiff (in civilian terms) will sit in a chair placed to the right of the bench. About three dozen metal folding chairs for spectators are arranged in rows at the back of the room.

Opposing counsels will have their places at two folding tables before the bench.

At 1215 hours, nearly an hour early, Evelyn Davis and her counsel, Captain Patrick Bailey, are already in their places at the defense table. Bailey wants his client to get used to the feel of the room before it is filled with intimidating people. He also needs to attend to a few last-minute items of business with Evelyn.

She is dressed in her Class A uniform, Army green with highly polished black low-quarter shoes. Bailey also wears Class As, but, after his usual fashion, his black tie is slightly askew, his brass is polished to only a low luster, and his shoes need a vigorous buffing.

"You look sharp," he told Evelyn. "That's important - not just to impress these officers, but so as not to make any contrast with Denise. If I know how the prosecutor operates, Rakes' gonna look like a magazine or a calendar photo. We want you to look just as good."

He catches Evelyn looking quizzically at his uniform and grins.

"Yeah, I know. I look like the dog slept on my uniform. That's part of the show; they have to respect my captain's bars, but they don't have to be impressed by how I look. You'll look even better next to me, and that's what we want."

A little after one p.m., the members of the military court begin to take their places. First in are the potential jurors: ten officers, two of whom are women. Bailey consults his juror list, comparing the names and ranks with the faces he sees at the table.

The panel is a fairly representative sample of the White Range officer corps: two full colonels, two lieutenant colonels, two majors, two captains, a first lieutenant and a second lieutenant. One captain and the second lieutenant are women. When the jury selection is complete, Bailey wants to have at least one woman.

He scans the list again to see how the officers stack up as to branch of service. Since the jury pool has been drawn from the personnel of a missile range, he isn't surprised to note that the preponderance of the officers is from the artillery. There is a scattering of other branches transportation, medical, finance and the like. Bailey is pleased to note that no infantry officers are included, and that none of the panel members is wearing combat patches on their right shoulders. His client does not need to undergo the judgment of hard-nosed infantrymen or men who have served in overseas combat zones. A service background with a little softer edge is what he wants.

While the jury panelists are taking their places, Bailey leans toward Evelyn and whispers: "You remember the drill here?"

"Yes, sir," she whispers back. "Sit up straight but not all stiff like I'm at attention. Look at whoever's talking. Don't react to what they say. If I don't understand something, make a note and ask you later. Try not to show emotion."

"That's a good soldier," Bailey says. "You'll do fine. And you look great."

In her uniform Evelyn could have passed inspection by a sergeant major of the Coldstream Guards. And, unusual among female soldiers, the Class A clothes flatter her figure. Her straight black hair — the legacy of her Native American ancestry is cut short, but not too short, and it makes an attractive frame for her appealing face.

The prosecution makes its appearance in the person of the lead counsel, Captain Michael L. Larson, and his assistant, Captain Michael L. Walters. Captain Larson is in his late thirties. His facial features are true to his Scandinavian heritage. Captain Walters is more a marine prototype: late twenties, solidly built, square jaw, and crew-cut hair. They greet and shake hands with Bailey, nod to Evelyn, and take their places at their table, piling it with paperwork.

The court reporter is like Evelyn, a Spec 4. She enters the room and sets up her stenographic machine at her small table. Then, the sergeant-at-arms comes in through a door behind the judge's desk and calls the room to attention.

The participants snap to it as the military judge, Lieutenant Colonel Gordon R. Denison, makes his entrance through the door. Judge Denison is in his late forties. His carriage and bearing command immediate respect. "As you were," he commands. Everyone sits down.

Trial lawyers don't like surprises, unless they are springing them themselves. Patrick Bailey doesn't expect any from Captain Mike Larson, who will present the government's case against Evelyn. Bailey knows Larson to be a no-nonsense litigator who'll make his case thoroughly and in a business-like military manner. Still, Bailey continues to be uneasy over the prospect that landmines lay in the path of his client in the person of Denise Rakes.

As the court-martial opens, Bailey has not yet had the opportunity to interview Rakes. He would have been more assured if he had a better idea of the direction her testimony will take. Rakes is the prosecution's chief witness. The testimony she gives about the killing of Angela Kinney will frame the case and determine the nature of the added defense he will have to mount on Evelyn's behalf. Bailey has already brought to the judge's attention the difficulty he is having in securing an interview with Rakes. He is largely in the dark as to the details she will present on the stand.

Now, with all the participants in place, the court is called to order by the judge. Larson opens the trial. He stands and reads from a prepared script: "This court is convened by Court-Martial Convening Order Number 2, Headquarters vs. United States Army White Sands Missile Range, New Mexico, as amended by Court-Martial Convening Order Number 4, Headquarters, U.S. Army White Sands Missile Range, New Mexico, a copy of which has been furnished to each member of the court."

Larson notes for the record that all members of the court, counsel and the defendant are present, and finishes the opening formalities, saying, "The prosecution is ready to proceed in the case of the United States against Specialist 4 Evelyn Davis, who is present in court."

Then it is the judge's turn. He apologizes to the prospective jurors for the 15-minute delay in opening the trial, then notes for the jury's benefit that Evelyn has had the option of having her case heard by a judge only, but had chosen to go before a jury. He also explains that she could have asked for the presence of enlisted personnel on the jury, but has agreed to be tried by a panel made up solely of officers.

After formally swearing in the potential jurors, Denison has the sergeant-at-arms give each a copy of preliminary instructions for their conduct. He emphasizes that these are provided merely for guidance, and that his oral instructions are to take precedence.

"It is my duty as military judge to ensure that this trial is conducted in a fair and orderly manner," the colonel says. "You are required to follow my instructions on the law and may not consult any other source as to the law pertaining to this case unless it is admitted into evidence. Any questions you may have should be asked of me in open court."

Bailey scribbles something on a legal pad and slides it over to Evelyn. "We know who's in charge. This guy is more than okay."

Denison next explains to the panelists that they will be subjected to *voir dire* examination by him and the opposing lawyers for the purpose of ascertaining whether any of them might be unable to judge the evidence impartially. He states there are two possible ways of disqualification of a member — a challenge for cause based on potential bias, or a peremptory challenge exercised by either side for which no reason has to be given.

"It is no adverse reflection upon a panel member to be excused from a particular case," the judge says, "Since the reasons for such a challenge, especially a peremptory challenge may be anything including a perceived mathematical advantage in a smaller court."

'Or if I just don't like your looks,' Bailey says to himself.

Denison takes a considerable amount of time to explain a function a military jury can exercise that a civilian jury cannot. A military jury can ask a direct questions to the witnesses.

He tells the jurors that they can write their questions to be asked of witnesses and submit them to him, being careful that no one else on the jury reads them. If he considers the jury questions to be appropriate, he will present them to witnesses. In any event, all the questions will be made part of the trial record. Jurors will be given the opportunity to call or recall witnesses.

Denison issues the usual warning to jurors about not discussing the case among themselves until it is time for their deliberations, and about not discussing the case with anyone else.

Denison finishes by laying out the trial schedule. "After these instructions, we will proceed to challenges and possible excusal of members, then opening statements by counsel, then presentation of evidence. After both sides have rested, there will be closing arguments of counsel. After the arguments, I will give you complete instructions on the law you are to apply in this case. Then you will retire to deliberate. After doing so you will announce your verdict."

He adds that if Evelyn is convicted of either or both of the charges against her, a sentencing proceeding will follow, in which the jury will also participate. "If there are no questions, we are ready to proceed to the general nature of the charges."

As the judge and the jury panel shuffle their growing stacks of paperwork into order, Bailey leans toward Evelyn. "That was a lot to sit through and you don't have to understand it all, but what it amounts to is that this judge is going to lean over backwards to see that you get a fair trial. He's gonna run this by the book."

Evelyn just nods.

Captain Larson stands again. "The general nature of the charges in this case is murder, a violation of Article 118, Uniform Code of Military Justice and accessory after the fact of murder, a violation of Article 78, Uniform Code of Military Justice." He briefly reviews the mechanics by which the charges are formulated and forwarded to the court.

Now, the stage is set for examination of the jury panel's qualifications. Because the missile range is a comparatively small community, Bailey expects that the *voir dire* will not be very far along before the first indication of potential partiality arises — and he is right.

Colonel Denison opens the examination by saying, "If any member of the court is aware of any matter that may be possible grounds for challenge by either side against him, he or she should now stipulate that."

One of the female captains raises her hand. "Specialist Davis has worked in my section at McAfee Health Clinic," the woman testifies. "She's attended meetings in my office and we have had one meeting behind closed doors."

The judge nods approvingly. "Thank you for that disclosure. Counsel may wish to talk to you about that in a moment."

"Any other disclosures?" the judge asks. "Apparently not. Does anyone else know this accused, Specialist Davis, seated here across the room from you?"

There is no response. "Apparently not."

The judge asks if any of the panelists knew or recognized the name of the victim, Angela Kinney. Again, there is no response.

Then the judge asks if the prosecution wishes to question the panelists.

"Your Honor," Mike Larson said, "the government is satisfied with the panel as set."

Bailey makes a mental note to the effect that Larson either has a good deal of confidence in his case, in the make-up of the jury panel, or both.

Turning to Bailey, Colonel Denison asks, "Does the defense wish to *voir dire*?"

"Yes, Your Honor."

"All right, I'll have some instructions on that before you begin. Do you think this is going to take a while?"

"Yes sir," Bailey replies. "We anticipate that it will."

"In that case, let's adjourn for this afternoon and start on your examination tomorrow morning. Everyone all right with that? Fine. Let's all be back here at 9:30 a.m. tomorrow morning. We are adjourned."

Everyone rises as the judge gets up and leaves the courtroom.

Bailey tucks his notepad into his briefcase and turns to Evelyn. "So far, so good," he tells her. "No damage, no surprises, Tomorrow I'm going to pick that jury apart like a Thanksgiving turkey. We'll end up with a few people we can work with, and take it from there."

Evelyn does not respond. Now that the court-martial has finally begun, she feels herself to be overwhelmed. What other people do and say in the next few days represent the determining forces against which she is utterly powerless.

Bailey senses her mood. "Remember that you know what really happened that night. I know it, and when this is over, they'll know it, too. Hold onto that thought."

The M.P. leads her back to her cell.

WHITE SANDS COURTROOM
19 OCTOBER 1983

This day is to be a test of patience and attentiveness for all the court-martial participants, for Pat Bailey lives up to his promise to put all the potential jurors under a microscope.

The proceedings are going to be particularly testing for Evelyn Davis. She has to maintain her composure and military bearing throughout. Before the court assembles in the morning, Bailey gives Evelyn a brief pep talk. "This is going to take a long time," he warns. "I need to get into these people's heads and find out things about them that some of them probably don't even know about themselves. It means some repetition, but it's really important. Just one person with a bad attitude or an ax to grind can make the difference. So, are you ready to sit through it?"

"I don't have much of a choice, do I?" Evelyn replies. Her voice is flat.

"Nope. We're all in this all the way. You just need to look sharp the way you did yesterday and you'll be fine. If you see or hear anything you think we ought to follow up on, you just make a note on this pad and I'll try to get to it."

Colonel Denison enters and takes his place. The second day begins. "Captain Bailey, you may *voir dire* the members."

Bailey stakes out a spot in front of the jurors' table and begins. "Thank you, Your Honor. Members of the court, you already heard who I am. Let me tell you a little bit about what I am. I'm the senior defense counsel with the United States Army Trial Defense Service assigned here. My office is responsible for handling criminal defense matters at White Sands Missile Range and I am the attorney for Specialist Davis who sits here accused of murder and accessory after the fact of murder."

"Now, the judge has asked you some preliminary questions and I have quite a few to go over, given the nature of the case and given the issues, and I appreciate all of your patience and putting up with this." He pauses, referring to the notes in his hand. "Has anyone on the panel heard about a murder case that occurred at White Sands?"

"No. Let me ask it this way: Is there anyone who hasn't heard about this case or heard of a murder case?" Only one hand goes up, from one of the lieutenant colonels. Bailey thinks to himself, '*I wonder what galaxy he's been living in.*'

"Thank you, sir. Now, let's go through this individually and ask each of you to just generally say what you heard about it, and when."

Except for the lieutenant colonel who professed ignorance of the case, all the members state that they have heard conversation about the killing, read about it in newspapers, or heard about it on television. Bailey considers that to be about par for the course; a happening as sensational as the Kinney slaying would have been grist for the rumor mill and the press in any community, let alone one as compact and inter-related as White Sands.

Bailey spends considerable time eliciting from each panelist what he or she knows about the case, and from what source, then, he goes to the heart of the matter.

"Now, for those members who indicate that they either saw things on television or read newspaper reports, what you heard about this case, have you drawn any conclusions about what happened?" He watches for a sign — a show of hands, an uncomfortable squirm, an aversion of gaze. '*Negative response*,' Bailey sums up.

"The reason I'm so concerned about it," he continues, "is that, without exception, I believe each one of you described this as a murder or crime." He pauses to let the panelists think about that, and then reminds them pointedly that their perception of murder or crime has not yet been founded on any evidence.

Bailey returns to the counsel table where he can make notes on individual responses and continues to the next round of questioning, asking each member in exhaustive detail whether he or she knows or has any kind of relationship with any of the participants in the trial.

Then he moves on to job descriptions. What does each of the panelists do on the post? What do their spouses do? Does their work bring them into contact with any of the trial participants?

He presses on. Do any of the panelists have any connection with the law enforcement functions of the military? Have any of them, personally or in their families, experienced any incidents involving violent crime? Have any of them participated in previous court-martials? What opinions do they have as to the level of punishment appropriate to violent crimes? Do any of them believe that it is imperative to reach a guilty verdict merely because someone died?

Satisfied with the information he has drawn out so far, Bailey next ventures onto what he knows to be "thin ice." Another one of the issues that's going to come up in this case is the issue of "lesbianism."

He begins. "I hate to throw terms around, but for right now let's leave it at that. You're going to find that several people involved in this case are gay and prefer women sexually."

He asks for frank responses to the following question and gets them. "Do you think homosexual relations may cause problems within a unit of my type in war and peacetime?"

"Would it pose a problem of morale and so forth within a unit of my type?"

"Do you consider it to be abnormal?"

"In the military, there are prohibitions against homosexuality. Do you support these prohibitions?"

"Could you not tolerate love affairs, heterosexual or homosexual, between members of the same unit because you lose all dispassionate objectivity if you've got lovers in the same organization?"

"From your military experience, does homosexuality create far too many problems for you to passively accept homosexuals, recognizing that there are homosexuals in the unit and that they're conducting themselves in a stellar manner and keeping their sexual feelings on a personal basis and out of the working commune?"

"Do you think homosexuality is abnormal behavior, but it would influence my decision in the trial?"

"Do you think that it should be condoned in the military?"

Overall, Bailey gets pretty much what he expects- a virtually unanimous disapproval of homosexuality in the military, and assertions that this disapproval wouldn't work against his client as far as the charges are concerned. The only surprise, a mildly reassuring one, is that Bailey does not detect among the jurors what he can identify as strong, closed-minded prejudice against gays as individuals. If homophobia lives in the panel, it is for now in the closet.

Taking a risk, he decides to press this consideration just a bit farther. "Is there any member of the panel who thinks that it would be impossible for a woman to love another woman both emotionally and sexually?"

He waits for a response. There is none.

"Do you all agree that the feelings between two women in that situation might be the same as the, let's say typical stereotype, of a man and woman in love?"

Bailey interprets the panel's nods and body language as an affirmative response, and decides he has pushed it far enough. He reasons that the officers do not want a thinly-disguised lecture on the psychology of homosexuality, and certainly do not want to hear a sermon on tolerance and liberality, at least not at this point. So he changes the subject to another consideration at the heart of Evelyn's defense. "Has any member of the panel not seen a situation where a person tries to cover up for someone else's behavior or misconduct?"

"Do you believe that being in love with someone might motivate a person to cover up for some of their misconduct; that that might be a situation where that cover-up happens?"

He doesn't get any definitive response to those questions; nor does he really want one. What he wants is to plant the seed of an idea.

Bailey's picking at the attitudes and perceptions of the jurors consumes the morning. When the court-martial recesses for lunch, he and Evelyn remain in the courtroom. He arranges for a sandwich lunch to be delivered, so that he and his client have a chance to talk privately and so that Evelyn is not taken back to her cell.

When they are again alone, Evelyn asks, "They don't like me, do they?"

"You can't say that," Bailey replied. "They might not like what you represent, a homosexual in the Army. But that's just a general feeling; it isn't necessarily directed at you personally. I don't think they either like or dislike you at all, at least where we are now. They see a criminal defendant whom they've sworn to give a fair trial."

"Maybe you're right; but I wish this was over."

"So do I," Bailey answers. "And it will be, soon enough. First, though, we have a lot of work to do. This afternoon we're going to get rid of some of these folks."

He explains that when the court reconvenes, he will issue his challenges to the prospective jurors, asking that they be removed. The judge will consider his challenges one at a time while the jurors are excused and waiting in another room. "I think we can remove three or four of these officers for cause because there are solid arguments against them. Then I'll have a chance to bounce one more without giving any reason at all"

"The prosecutor also can issue challenges for cause and remove one juror without giving a reason." Bailey doubts that Larson will do so. The prosecutor already has already indicated that the jury panel is acceptable to him. For the rest of the lunch break, Bailey and his client visit about life outside the courtroom, although for neither of them is that life outside the court room of great interest on this day.

When the court-martial reconvenes for the afternoon session, the judge asks both sides if any business needs to be transacted before the challenges are presented.

It is the prosecution's prerogative to issue the first challenge. Contrary to what Bailey has told Evelyn, Captain Mike Larson does voice an objection to one of the potential jurors: a captain who is one of the two women on the panel. Bailey winces inwardly. He had hoped to keep this woman.

Larson points out that the woman had said she worked at the health clinic with Evelyn and had perceived in her demeanor signs of hostility. He also notes that the captain had expressed some compassion for the situation Evelyn was in.

"It appears," Larson said, "that to some extent she has emotions that may pull her both ways, but still do not necessarily leave her in the middle as a disinterested member of the panel. We think that in the best interest of justice, she should not sit on this panel."

Colonel Denison looks at Bailey. "Do you wish to be heard on that?"

"Yes sir." Bailey stood. "As counsel has indicated in his argument, the only prejudice that would result in leaving this member on the panel, if any, would probably be against the accused."

He repeats what Larson has just said about the captain having identified feelings of hostility in their mutual workplace, then says Evelyn will specifically waive any right she has to challenge the woman.

This is the first dilemma the judge has to confront. He does so decisively: "The member has indicated that she's willing and able to disregard her prior knowledge of this case. I'm satisfied that she is a qualified and impartial juror. The challenge is denied."

Bailey sits down next to Evelyn and scrawls a note. "You one; them zero."

Larson said he has no other challenges, and it is Bailey's turn. He starts with the senior colonel on the panel. Consulting his notes, he reminds the judge that this officer is well acquainted with Denise Rakes, the principal prosecution witness. In Bailey's examination, the colonel had said Rakes was his 'favorite bartender' at the Officers' Club; that he had participated in a proceeding which resulted in Rakes being barred from

White Sands Officer's Club because of the 'catfight'; that he had consulted with Rakes' husband, Vance, about a compassionate reassignment to other duty; that he had a personal and official relationship with the prosecutor, Mike Larson, and that he had been involved in the Army's relocation of Evelyn's children to Omaha after she was incarcerated.

It's a damning list, and although Larson goes through the motions of opposing the challenge, the judge sustains Bailey's objections and the colonel is taken off the panel.

Next Bailey turns his guns on one of the lieutenant colonels. "First, this officer has said that he also knows Denise Rakes. He has had business dealings with her owing to her part-time job at a local bank. At one time Rakes had done him an important personal favor in straightening out a bounced check. Secondly, the officer has complained that his participation in the court-martial would get in the way of his preparation for an inspector-general's inspection of his office. Finally, the colonel has admitted to hearing through the grapevine about weird sexual things in connection with the case."

The judge also grants this challenge.

Working his way downward by rank, Bailey then issues a challenge to a major who is the post's public affairs officer. His duties include preparing statements for the press about Evelyn's case, which, Bailey said, gives him access to information which can be prejudicial and not covered in the expected testimony. The major is also one of the officers who stated that being homosexual is abnormal."

The judge dismisses the major. The panel is now down to 7 members.

Bailey isn't finished. Next he seeks the removal of the male captain on the list, on grounds that the captain has admitted to hearing several rumors about the case and that he, too, knows Denise Rakes in her capacity as a bartender at the Officer's Club.

The prosecutor leaps to the captain's defense, and this time Colonel Denison agrees with the Army. The captain stays. Bailey is only mildly disappointed.

Bailey loses on his next challenge, too. He tries to disqualify a first lieutenant who has had civilian training and experience in law enforcement. Bailey's objection is that this background could cause the juror to give more than equal weight to prosecution testimony by M.P.s and civilian policemen. He also contends that since the lieutenant has had some investigative training himself, he might be drawn to make his own conclusions about the evidence, rather than be guided by the judge's instructions.

The challenge is denied.

This brings the challenges for cause to an end. All that remains in the jury selection is the exercise of peremptory challenges by both sides.

Larson objects to the presence on the panel of the female second lieutenant. Bailey frowns; he had wanted both women to remain. But a peremptory challenge cannot be argued.

Bailey uses his peremptory challenge to remove the remaining major.

The jury is complete. It is down to five members: a colonel, who by rank will serve as foreman; one lieutenant colonel; two captains, and a first lieutenant. One woman remains.

The judge calls a brief recess. Bailey uses the time to tell a sullen Evelyn that the jury is the best they could have hoped for.

Evelyn asks "but I wonder why you didn't say anything about me being black and all them being white?"

"Because I don't want to get into that," Bailey replies.

He explains that race is not an important factor in the trial. All three main figures are black. "We don't have a black-on-white situation here or a white-on-black.The Army prides itself on being more racially tolerant and integrated than the rest of the society. Putting a racial spin on this trial could hurt our case.

After the recess, Bailey addresses the court. While the jury is absent, Bailey tackles a make-or-break issue for his client: the damning role that Denise Rakes will play with her testimony.

"Maybe it's appropriate now, Your Honor, to bring up the problem of the testimony of Mrs. Rakes."

The judge makes no indication that it isn't appropriate. Bailey draws a deep breath and proceeds. "She's evidently informed trial counsel that she refused to interview with the defense. We request that she not be allowed to testify. Her failure to grant us an interview, either prior to or after her direct examination, amounts to a denial of my client's constitutional rights to confront and cross-examine the witnesses against her."

Denison raises an eyebrow. "You're asking me to prevent her from testifying?"

"She did not consent to an interview by the defense either before her direct examination or after. Yes, sir. We cannot effectively cross-examine and confront a witness who declines to be interviewed."

Bailey knows he is stretching his point. The right of a defendant to confront accusers is covered by the cross-examination process in open court; the defense's attempt to prevent Rakes from testifying probably reaches beyond the reasonable. But it's worth a try. If by some chance the judge blocks Rakes' testimony, the bulk of the Army's case disappears.

The judge goes right to the heart of the matter. "Doesn't she have a right to refuse to consent to an interview if she wishes?"

"I would agree with that statement, Your Honor," Bailey says. "But again, when it comes down to weighing the right of a witness who refuses to interview with the defense against an accused's right to confront and cross-examine witnesses against them, the rights of the accused should prevail. The only remedy available to this court is to not allow the witness to testify against the accused."

"Do you have any evidence" the judge asks, "or are you making any allegation of prosecutorial misconduct?"

"No, sir, I am not."

"Are you contending that anybody has improperly told her that she has a right to refuse, or influenced her to refuse by a member of the prosecution's staff?"

Bailey knows that he will be opening a can of worms, or, more accurately, a barrel of snakes, if he gives any indication that he suspects Mike Larson of improper legal conduct, so he phrases his reply carefully. "I have no information that would show any kind of prosecutorial misconduct."

The judge turns to Larson and asks him to respond to Bailey's request.

The prosecutor argues exactly as Bailey expected him to. Evelyn's right to confrontation under the Sixth Amendment will not be harmed by Rakes' refusal to be interviewed prior to her testimony. "In fact," Larson states, "the prosecution has gone out of its way, within the bounds of professional responsibility, short of advising Mrs. Rakes to speak to Captain Bailey, to try and get her to do that. She elected not to do so, all on the advice of her counsel."

He points out that when Rakes testifies, Bailey will have the opportunity to cross-examine her, which fulfills the right of confrontation. He also reminds the judge that Bailey has had access to Rakes' initial statements in the case for several months, and that they provide adequate basis for preparing a cross-examination.

Bailey knows he can't argue effectively against the prosecution's contention, and doesn't try.

The judge announces his decision: "I would not hesitate to interfere judicially if there were any allegation or evidence of prosecutorial misconduct in misadvising this witness, but, from all that I have before me, it appears that she is aware of her rights. The witness has the right to decline to be interviewed before trial."

To Bailey, "Your request that I prevent Denise Rakes from testifying is denied."

Denison asks if either side has any further business to address, then adjourns the court until the following morning when the jury will begin hearing the evidence against Evelyn Davis.

WHITE SANDS MISSILE RANGE
20 OCTOBER 1983

The headlines of the morning paper read:
G.I. MURDER TRIAL
OPENS AT WHITE SANDS
Opening statements by attorneys
are expected today in the court-martial
of a servicewoman accused of the
strangulation killing of another
woman soldier at White Sands
last April 7.
Charged with first-degree
murder is Spec. 4 Evelyn Davis,
in a case tinged with elements of
Satanism, occult rites, lesbianism
and sado-masochism.

"Damn it" Colonel Mark Silverstine mutters into his coffee cup as he read the morning paper's coverage of Evelyn's court-martial.

The Army believes in supporting the press's First Amendment rights only up to the point at which the Army's interests may be compromised; then the lid goes on. Because White Sands is a missile base where sensitive technological data and equipment are kept, its security is tighter than an armored post or basic training center. Silverstine's M.P.s and the post's public affairs apparatus have done a good job of providing the local media with enough to satisfy editors and reporters, but not enough to encourage lurid reporting of the Angela Kinney murder. But now the press is talking about Satanism. "Lieutenant, get in here!"

Lieutenant Abel Stone responds immediately to Silverstine's tone of voice.

"We've got a goddamn boy scout in a cop's uniform creating a problem. Get every reporter off the base, and now!"

"But sir, what do I tell them?"

Silverstein's fist forcefully bangs the top of his desk, causing a small statue to fall over. "The magic words, National Security!"

WHITE SANDS COURTROOM
21 OCTOBER 1983

When the court-martial convenes, two new pieces of furniture have been added: a padded chair, and in front of it a small writing desk. This will be the witness stand.

"Be seated, please," Colonel Denison says as he makes his entrance. "Court will come to order."

He looks around the courtroom. "Let the record reflect that the five members of the jury are present, the other members of the panel having departed."

To the jury, "I described the challenge procedure to you during the preliminary instructions, and it is as a result of those proceedings that half of you are gone."

"Under the law, the accused is presumed to be innocent of any of the offenses against her. The government has the burden of proving this accused's guilt, if it can, beyond a reasonable doubt. The fact that these charges have been alleged against this accused and referred to this court for trial does not permit any inference of her guilt".

"You must make your determination of the guilt or innocence of this accused based solely upon the evidence presented here in court and on the instructions which I will give you. Since you cannot properly make that decision until you have heard all the evidence and received my instructions, it is of vital importance that you keep an open mind until all the evidence has been presented to you and you have been fully instructed."

Bailey considers that in some lawyers' opinions, the judge is going overboard in redundantly cautioning the jury about its obligations regarding impartiality and fairness. He might have been a little bored by it himself, except that every word the judge says about the presumption of Evelyn's innocence is music to his ears.

Denison then instructs Captain Mike Larson to deliver the prosecution's opening statement.

Larson stands before the juror's bench and begins. "Members of the court, in the preliminary sessions, through *voir dire*, the reading of the charge sheet, the paperwork we've been through, you're aware of the charges against the accused: they are murder with premeditation by means of strangulation. The charges allege that Specialist Davis, the accused, murdered Angela

Collette Kinney, a Specialist Four assigned to the 62nd Transportation Company, Fort Bliss, Texas, by means of strangulation and that she did so with premeditation".

"Additionally, she's charged with, in the event that she had no part in the actual murder of Angela Kinney, that she assisted another individual, Denise Louise Rakes, in transporting the body from White Sands Missile Range to a place in the northeastern portion of El Paso, Texas, with the intent to avoid the prosecution or discovery of the crime."

Larson looks up from his notes. Establishing eye contact with the jurors, he continues. "I will not even begin to assert to you that just because the accused has been so charged she is guilty; there would he no reason for us to be here if that were true. You serve a very important function in the scheme of military justice. I also have a function in the scheme of military justice — that is, as the trial counsel. It is my job to provide to you the evidence that the government has discovered within the bounds of the Constitution and the Universal Code of Military Justice. Then the defense counsel, a well-qualified attorney, a member of the bar, well-experienced in the JAG Corps, can present his side of the case so that you may compare the two of them."

"I ask nothing more than your attention to the matters presented by both sides."

Larson walks back to the prosecution table and picks up a fresh set of notes. He takes a sip of water, then, returns to his spot in front of the jury.

'Okay' Bailey says to himself, *'if he's gonna load the boat, this is when it happens.'*

He knows that Larson is fair and professional as well as capable; but it is always hard for a prosecutor not to begin arguing his case in the opening statement. If Larson wants to start planting prejudicial ideas in the jurors' minds, he will do it now, putting a sinister spin on what should be a straightforward recitation of what the government hopes to prove.

Bailey has warned Evelyn that in the opening statement, Larson might try to make her look as evil and violent as he can get by with. She is not to say anything. She can register emotions through her facial expressions and body language. "It's all right to shake your head if he says something you know isn't true. It's all right to whisper to me, or write me notes. And it's all right to cry if you feel like it. The judge and jury will not mind any genuine expression of emotion."

So far in the trial, Evelyn has been a near perfect defendant, sitting straight in her chair, following the lawyers' discussion alertly, not giving the jurors any visible reason to render an unfavorable judgment of her demeanor. Now she nods to Bailey, indicating that she remembers his advice and is ready to hear the worst the prosecution has to offer.

"Members of this court," Larson says, opening scene two of his presentation, "You'll hear from a private. He's just a private, just a cook in a mess hail down at Fort Bliss. He will establish a relationship for you between the accused and the victim, Angela Kinney."

Larson pauses for effect. Bailey knows what is coming next.

"And you will hear from someone you have heard about quite a bit at this court-martial: You will hear from Denise Louise Rakes."

The prosecutor explains that Mrs. Rakes was arrested by the El Paso police at the same time as Evelyn, and that she originally had been a suspect in the murder of Angela Kinney. Rakes will appear before the court not as a defendant charged with murder but as an important witness against Evelyn. "I should tell you that she will come before you with a grant of immunity from prosecution. She has the right to assert her rights against self-incrimination, under the Fifth Amendment. She can give testimony here under the circumstance that any self-incriminating statements she might make are effectively immunized. That was done for a reason: so that you may hear what an eyewitness to the crime has to say."

Larson outlines the boundaries of Rakes' immunity. "Yes, she's a suspect in the murder. She is a suspect; she may very well be a suspect again. She has not yet been tried, but that does not mean that she cannot be tried. Anything she says in this courtroom cannot be used against her. That does not mean that any evidence already gathered cannot be used against her. She's not a free person necessarily. Don't consider her one. She hasn't beaten the rap and she's aware of it."

Bailey breathes a silent sigh of relief. Larson has just done part of his job for him in giving the jury a good reason to be skeptical of Rakes' testimony. Larson could have explained the circumstances of Rakes' immunity without going quite so far in portraying her as a witness who'd sink her friend and lover in order to save her own skin. Bailey makes a mental note that this may make a good point in his closing argument — that even the government's lawyer concedes that Rakes has a lot to gain with her testimony.

"Denise Rakes," Larson continues, "will describe to you with some detail what happened at 413 Vanguard on the night of the 7th of April 1983. You'll hear from the detective who took her confession in the early morning hours of the 13th of April 1983 and who was involved in this case, from the minute the sanitation workers found her body lying on the side of the road on that snowy morning in April. You'll hear how the investigation progressed. You'll hear that the cause of death was by strangulation."

Then, he tells the jurors, they'll hear testimony from the FBI as to the murder weapon and the evidence by which it is established as such. Larson returns to the counsel table and puts down his notes. He turns to the jury, to wrap up his opening remarks.

In conclusion, Larson merely says: "Representing the United States government, I ask only that you exercise your responsibilities under the code, that you listen to what is put before you and that you evaluate all evidence as fairly as possible. When you have done that, under the instructions you'll receive from the military judge, I'm convinced that you will have no alternative to a verdict of guilty as charged."

Before beginning his own opening remarks, Bailey whispers to Evelyn: "So far, so good." Again, no visible response.

Most trial lawyers like to work close to the jury, standing in front of the box and addressing individual members as if letting them in on closely guarded legal secrets.

Pat Bailey has a different idea in trying court-martials. He reasons that career military officers will find it more professional, hence more persuasive, to be addressed at a more formal level. So instead of approaching the jurors to establish a spurious intimacy, he stands at his place at the defense table and begins, speaking without notes. "Captain Larson has just given you a succinct overview of what this case is about, and I compliment him on it. In my remarks, I will touch briefly on two aspects of his presentation: what he said, and what he didn't say."

"What he didn't say is that the prosecution will provide tangible, material, physical evidence of Specialist Davis's guilt. You'll recall that he doesn't talk about fingerprints, tracks in the snow, tell-tale marks that can be traced back to the defendant. He sets the stage for the testimony his witnesses will give — but you will have noticed that none of these witnesses, except one, have any direct knowledge of what happened in that house that night."

"This brings us to what he did say and it is the most important aspect of this case: that you will hear the testimony of a witness whose own culpability in this matter has been firmly established. I refer to Denise Rakes. As Captain Larson indicated, her testimony is so important to the prosecution that she has been given a grant of immunity in order to be made willing to testify. I don't think that I need to emphasize that this circumstance must be regarded as casting a dark cloud on her veracity. In fact, Captain Larson has acknowledged as much, and I compliment him on that, also."

Bailey nods toward the prosecution table. "The government has been frank and candid about how Mrs. Rakes came to testimony in this case, and I don't want to create the impression that the prosecution is in any way trying to deal from the bottom of the deck. They are working with what they have."

Bailey pauses, raising a finger as if in admonition. "What they have isn't much, but I want you to listen carefully to it anyway, especially the statements of Mrs. Rakes. Even though her testimony may be seen as gravely damaging to my client, I think you should pay particular attention to it, and to the way it's presented. Ask yourselves if this person has a reason for saying what she will say and what that reason might be. Consider her demeanor on the witness stand. Listen analytically to the manner and content of her responses to questions asked by Captain Larson, myself and, perhaps, the judge."

"Then, please watch and listen just as closely when the defendant, Specialist Davis, is on the stand. And ask yourselves the same questions you had about her accuser's testimony. At this time I choose not to give you a preview of defense evidence, mainly because the defense has nothing to prove. I remind you that the entire burden of proof is on the prosecution. Specialist Davis is to be considered innocent until and unless the Army can prove her guilt beyond a reasonable doubt."

"Colonel Denison will instruct you as to the meaning of reasonable doubt. You will have no trouble finding it. Thank you."

Bailey sits down, giving Evelyn a reassuring nod.

As Mike Larson has promised in his opening statement, the prosecution's first witness is an Army private whose function is to establish a relationship between Evelyn Davis and the victim, Angela Kinney.

Private Reginald Gibbens, a good-looking, 22 year-old cook who had been in the Army 14 months, states that he became acquainted with Kinney while they lived in the same billets at Fort Bliss. They met about three weeks before Kinney's death while they were watching television in the unit dayroom and progressed to several dinner dates.

One night, Gibbens relates that two female soldiers came to the billets to pick up Angela Kinney. She introduced them to him.

Larson asks, "Did you learn that one of them named was Specialist Davis?"

"No sir. She was introduced to me as Bandit, sir."

"So she went by the name Bandit?"

"Yes, sir,"

Gibbens then points out Evelyn as the woman he had met as Bandit. Angela Kinney had told him she and Bandit were friends.

The point having been made that Evelyn and Kinney were closely associated, Larson turns Gibbens over to Pat Bailey for cross-examination.

"Angela Kinney was gay, was she not?"

"I don't know. She didn't tell me, sir."

"Given what you think."

"I would think so, sir."

"One more question. Angela Kinney wasn't stupid, was she?"

"No sir."

Bailey has no further questions, and Gibbens is excused.

Bailey isn't sure why Larson had called the private to the stand just to get on the record that Evelyn and Kinney knew each other; that much could have been established by virtually any of the other prosecution witnesses. Bailey might have chosen a more dramatic approach to keep the jury interested, but then, he reflects, these are military officers and may appreciate a presentation that marches in orderly formation.

Larson's assistant counsel, Captain Michael L. Walters, takes the next witness, Detective Ray Martinez of the El Paso Police Department.

Martinez describes being sent to the remote area where Kinney's body was discovered and being assigned to conduct a preliminary investigation of the site. "As I walked up to the body it appeared to be that of a relatively young age, black female. She was wearing a T-shirt and blue Levi pants; they appeared to be new. She had white high-top tennis shoes on. The soles of the shoes, upon examination, were free of any kind of debris. Based on the surrounding area, very sandy and very moist, it didn't appear that the shoes, other than the heels had come in contact with the dirt."

Martinez states that this led him to believe that Kinney's body had been carried to where it was found. "She was lying with her feet pointing in an easterly direction," he continued. "As I got down to the body, I could see that there were some scratch marks around the neck. They appeared to be abrasions around the upper portion of the neck in the back and the lower portion of the neck in the front."

Next Walters shows Martinez another photograph: a close-up of Kinney's head, shoulders, and chest, showing more of the abrasions around her neck.

Martinez tells the court that the body had no jewelry or identification, no money or wallet. He did find a slip of paper in the watch pocket of the jeans on which were written phone numbers which turned out to be those of a Larry Miles and Angela's husband, Tony Kinney.

Then Walters asks Martinez to walk the jury through the autopsy which had been performed at an El Paso hospital.

Colonel Denison interrupts. "A moment, Captain. Wouldn't it be the usual procedure to call the medical examiner or coroner and have him present evidence relating to the autopsy?"

"Yes, sir, it would," Walters replies, "but the autopsy was relatively simple and straightforward, and we thought it would save time to have Detective Martinez report on it; he was there. And, I believe the defense will stipulate to the officer's testimony?"

He looks at Bailey for confirmation.

Bailey nods. "The defense is familiar with this evidence, your honor, and has no objection to it being presented by this witness."

"Go ahead, detective," Walters said. "What happened at the hospital?"

"The medical examiner made a second liver probe to determine body temperature at that time. He determined it to be 63.5 degrees Fahrenheit. Her clothes were then removed, and I noticed that she had defecated extensively in her underwear and in her jeans."

Walters asks Martinez if his experience led him to draw any conclusions from this.

"Yes sir. Many times when you have a violent, struggling type death, the person will defecate during the attack. In any kind of death, the releasing of the bowels is that of a comparatively light spotting in the underwear: not of the magnitude found in this victim's clothing."

Walters asks Martinez to describe what the kind of death which would have produced this result.

"Where the individual knows death is imminent," the detective states. "and they are struggling to free themselves from a great deal of pain and fear of death." He then identifies a prosecution exhibit, a photograph taken in the course of the autopsy which shows ligature markings on her neck as her skin dried out in the hospital.

"Now," Waiters asks, "did the medical examiner tell you the cause of this victim's death?"

"Yes sir."

"And what did he say'?"

"We were advised that the young lady had been strangled to death."

Walters pauses for a moment to give that a chance to imprint on the jurors, and then continues. "Now, detective, how did you continue your investigation after the autopsy?"

"At that time she had no identification on her person," Martinez replies.

"So how did you finally identify her?"

"In cooperation with the Army, inquiries were made as to whether there were any black females that were missing from the barracks or listed AWOL or gone for any period of time. The 62nd Transportation Company had such an individual. Also, the unit had received a phone call inquiring as to this individual's whereabouts. The first sergeant of the unit and a warrant officer went to the hospital and made a visual identification of the body."

Bailey rises to say, "The defense has no objection to this line of questioning and testimony, but would ask that it be noted in the record that the witness is submitting evidence that was gathered by an agency other than his own. The Army investigators are not here to present what they found; the witness is doing it for then. We expect that as this matter proceeds, there will be further such presentations, second-hand testimony that could be labeled as hearsay. This is acceptable to the defense as long as it is kept within bounds and we certainly will enter our objection if it isn't."

"So noted," Denison says. "The prosecution is advised that in the interest of simplicity and saving time, a certain amount of summarized or hearsay testimony will be accepted, as it was just now with the coroner's findings."

Walters continues. "Did your investigation give you any indication who may have been involved in the death of Angela Kinney?"

Martinez tells the jury that the Army and the El Paso P.D. established that a Davis was closely linked to the victim. On further inquiry, the detective states, Bandit and Davis turned out to be the same person, and another woman, Denise Rakes, was added to the list of witnesses or suspects.

Then Martinez describes his questioning of Evelyn.

"She became very agitated, extremely nervous. It was difficult for her to talk. She had to clear her throat several times and appeared totally - very upset."

Walters doesn't ask Martinez to provide the substance of what Evelyn said in her questioning: a transcript of her statement having been previously provided to the jury.

Bailey takes over on cross-examination. "Now, one of the techniques you used to get the statement from Specialist Davis was that you went in and told her, 'Hey, Rakes is laying all this on you.' Right?"

Martinez shakes his head, "That was not a technique. That was something that occurred."

"All right," Bailey said. "So one of the things you did say to her was, 'Hey, Rakes is laying all this on you, you better hurry up and tell us what really happened,' right? Something along those lines?"

"Something along those lines."

"Okay. And isn't it a fact that she was quite concerned over and upset about Denise Rakes? Didn't she ask to see Denise Rakes?"

"Yes. She said something to the effect that she would talk to me only if I would let her see Mrs. Rakes.

Bailey says that he has just one more question:" Why did you tell Specialist Davis that Denise Rakes was blaming it on her?"

The detective replies, "Because in her interrogation, Mrs. Rakes said, 'Well, it was she who did it, she's the one that did everything.' So I told Davis."

The judge calls a brief recess.

While the jurors are out, Bailey asks Evelyn how she is doing.

"I don't know. They'll all believe what Denise says when she says it again."

"Don't worry about that yet," Bailey says. "One thing at a time. We'll get a chance to nibble at her credibility before she even testifies. I've got some things in store for her when she takes the stand."

He pauses for a long moment, before telling Evelyn "We're gonna have to show the jury that you were trying to protect Denise."

Evelyn replies. "I thought I was doing the right thing and maybe I still do."

When the court reconvenes, the prosecution resumes with Captain Larson now at the helm and Ray Martinez still on the stand.

"Sergeant," Bailey resumes, "I have a question I'd like you to answer based on your experience as a police officer and your involvement in the early stages of this case. Did anything strike you as unusual about the questioning of Evelyn Davis on the night she was taken into custody?"

Martinez looks at Mike Larson, expecting the prosecutor to object to such a broad question. Larson is silent. Martinez answers. "First, I'd have to say that her statements didn't quite ring true. I don't think she was telling the whole story."

"In what regard?" Bailey interjects,

"I can't say for sure," Martinez continues, "but I got the impression from her demeanor and her very apparent concern for what was going on with Denise Rakes that she was either holding something back or changing the emphasis of her story. I don't know."

"Anything else?"

"Yes sir. At the time, I wondered about how much in a hurry we were to get Rakes' story down, grant her immunity and zero in on Specialist Davis as the prime suspect."

"Did you share these concerns with anyone else?" Bailey asks.

"Well, not specifically, as I recall. It was just a feeling I had."

Bailey tries another tact. "In the course of this proceeding, the defendant was arraigned in the Federal District Court in El Paso. I believe you were present at that arraignment, even though you were not called to testify and had no official role there. And at the beginning of this court-martial, I believe you also were present in the room. Why was that?"

Martinez shifts in his chair." Well, I'm always interested in the processing of cases I'm involved in. And I guess I'd have to say that the aspects of this case that I've just mentioned were bothering me some."

Bailey moves closer to the witness chair. "Then let me see if we can sum this up. You've testified that in the course of questioning Specialist Davis and Mrs. Rakes, you became aware or at least suspicious, that something outside of the ordinary was going on. And you have testified that you thought, perhaps, Specialist Davis had some hidden motivation in the statement she gave. Further, you say you were bothered by the apparent haste with which Mrs. Rakes was dismissed and the defendant was charged with the crime."

Bailey pauses and looks at the jury. Turning back to Martinez, he asks: "In your opinion, detective, are the Army and Mrs. Rakes trying to frame Evelyn Davis?"

Larson jumps up with the objection Bailey knows is coming.

"Sustained," Colonel Denison snapped. "We don't need the witness's opinion; guilt or innocence is for the jury to decide."

"No further questions."

After this exchange, Mike Larson knows that some damage control is in order. In redirect, he asks Martinez: "Detective, you've indicated here today that you had what might be called misgivings about the processing of this case, is that correct."

"Yes sir. I guess you could say that."

"Let me ask you: have you reported these misgivings to your superior officers in the police department. or to the U.S. district attorney or to any official of the Army at White Sands or at Fort Bliss'?"

"No sir, I haven't."

"A final question, Detective: have you witnessed, or been told about, any investigative misconduct or prosecutorial misconduct in the handling of this case?"

"No sir. I have not."

Neither Larson nor Bailey has anything else for Martinez. When he steps down, the judge recesses for lunch.

The only witness in the afternoon session is an M.P. who had been on road patrol duty at White Sands the night of the killing.

Specialist 4 Stuart Bozer testifies that he and his partner saw two cars leaving the post. The movement of the second car aroused their suspicion because it seemed to be going abnormally slow. Bozer states that he followed the car and clocked it on radar at no faster than

35 miles an hour for some distance after leaving the post gate. Because he knew that slow, cautious driving often marked the conduct of a motorist who had been drinking and didn't want to attract attention, Bozer stopped the car and asked the driver to get out. He identified the driver as Evelyn Davis.

From observation, the M.P. could tell she had not been drinking, seemed calm and possessed, and apparently was not under the influence of any medication. After checking her driver's license and vehicle registration, he sent her on her way.

FORT BLISS, TEXAS
21 OCTOBER 1983

"You've got yourself quite a trial there, Patrick Bailey," Dr. Ellis says as he closes the file he'd been reading. And knowing you, you didn't give it to me just for casual reading."

Major Robert Ellis, M.D. is a career psychiatrist attached to the Bliss post hospital. He and Bailey are more than just Officers' Club acquaintances. Bailey has called on Ellis's medical expertise more than once in his work. Now he has given the doctor a summary of Evelyn's case, saying he needs more information on diverse sexual preferences than he can muster on his own.

"Yeah, it's more than light reading," Bailey said. "It may be an important element in this girl's defense. And there's more. Here."

He hands Ellis a two page document written on yellow legal pad paper. "Her mother sent me this poem."

Ellis scans the poem. "Well, leaving out the mother-daughter stuff, this would appear to be the writings of an acutely confused individual. She refers to herself as a man. There are references to 'my woman,' somebody she seems to be obsessed with protecting. That's the way you read it?"

Nodding, Bailey inquires, "What I want to know is, is Evelyn Davis a female, or do you think she could convince a jury she really is a male/female?"

Ellis lights a pipe and blows out a large cloud of fragrant smoke before sitting down at his desk. Bailey selects a large over-stuffed chair near the desk. "It isn't that simple. You don't just divide the world into boys and girls, or boys who want to be girls, or vice versa. I'll try to give you a little lecture. Let's call it Sexology 101."

It turns out to be more than a simple introductory lecture; more like Sexology 505. Bailey takes notes and tries to keep up with the doctor's discussion.

Ellis explains that what an individual becomes phenotypically can be influenced by factors other than an X or Y chromosome, the usually perceived determinant of gender. Up to about five or six weeks, female and male embryos are morphologically identical, each with the potential to develop male or female sexual organs. The clitoris is embryo logically the same as the penis. The fetus's own sex hormones determine which gender-specific reproductive organs are developed.

"You with me so far?"

"I think so," Bailey replies. "What you're saying is that in its early stages an embryo can go either way—male or female,"

"That's about right," Ellis confirms. "I'll get more specific. The absence of an enzyme called five alpha-reductase, the absence being a mistake on Nature's part, will cause a male fetus to be born phenotypically a female. These individuals remain females to all intents and purposes, until puberty, at which time they become phenotypically males,"

"You mean that a person without this alpha-whatever can be born as a boy and then turn into a girl?"

"That's close enough. And what's interesting is that the transition usually is made with minimal problems. Although they have been born, cast, and treated as females, inside they have always considered themselves males. They don't know why; it's just there."

He pauses to relight his pipe. "Let me give you a little more medical mumbo-jumbo if you can handle it."

"Go ahead. This is fascinating,"

Ellis continues, explaining that some male fetuses lack the enzyme which converts the male hormone, testosterone, into its active form, dihydrotestosterone. This is a genetic inborn error; it results in a relative insensitivity to androgens, and can result in male newborns and infants being phenotypically cast as females.

"Now, getting down to your case, you've shown me this girl's birth records. They indicate that she was what is termed an intersex baby. That is, she had ambiguous or both sets of external sexual organs. That would seem to explain why the birth records were withheld and safeguarded. By the way, I'm curious as to how you obtained them."

Bailey waves off the question. "I'd tell you if I knew. They were in an envelope that somebody placed in my car one night. I'm guessing that somebody had a pipeline into the hospital, pulled in some chits, or put the heat on somebody. It doesn't matter. I can't use this stuff in court if I can't identify the source."

Ellis raises an eyebrow. "You can't use it? Why then do you need to know so much about the subject?"

"If Evelyn is a male/female, I may find a way to get this sexual stuff in front of the jury, it might go to motive and character, and may count as a mitigating factor. At least, it will help me understand what I'm dealing with here."

"That sounds fair enough," Ellis replies. "Incidentally, I don't think you're committing any kind of legal slash medical malpractice by having that file in your possession. It isn't necessarily some deep, dark secret that can never be revealed."

He tells Bailey that society always has felt compelled to establish gender identity quickly after birth. The prevailing opinion is that socialization governs personality development and consequently, the genital organs of a baby have to correspond to the sexual identity chosen for it. For the psychological well-being of the child, it is argued that the identity needs to be established as soon as possible.

"I figure that's why the hospital sealed the records. It wasn't a conspiracy or a fear of lawsuits. It's just the S.O.P., standard operative procedure, for sexually ambiguous babies. If you look through records of any sizable hospital, I bet you'll find others."

"What else should I know about all this?" Bailey asks.

"Well," Ellis answers, "you get into areas of opinion and interpretation. For example, some of us don't subscribe to the concept that environmental considerations govern gender expression."

"What does that mean?"

"It means that the common impression that surroundings, upbringing, peer pressure and the like determine sexual preference isn't necessarily right."

"Off the record, there is good scientific data that indicate if you expose a female fetus to a testosterone-like hormone very early in the pregnancy, something called virilization of the brain occurs. This would make a female with XX for chromosomes act in life as if she were a male. Now, if you give a large dose of female hormone to a male fetus, you can create an XY female."

Bailey holds up a hand. "Wait a minute. You're talking about giving hormones or something to a fetus. How does that happen, and why?"

Ellis explained that in the '50s and '60s, it was a common practice for physicians to administer hormones to women with threatened abortions. Depending on when in gestation they are used and what kind of hormones they are administered, the potential for gender modification is created

"Do you think Evelyn Davis is a hermaphrodite: both man and woman?" Bailey asks.

"Probably not. She never identified herself as a girl. Biologically, she is probably a girl and everyone treated her like a girl, but inside, for all practical purposes, she has been wired as a male."

This brings up one of the main questions Bailey wants answered. "Evelyn has implied that she thinks she's a man trapped in a woman's body. Can that description be even halfway accurate?"

Ellis nods. "It could be totally accurate. You know, that's a common expression among homosexuals, a man trapped in a woman's body or vice versa. Nobody gives it much credence. They tend to write it off as just a far-fetched excuse or rationalization. But in physiological terms, it's real. Based on Cecilia's Riley's prenatal records, I'd lay pretty good odds that your client fits right in."

"All right," Bailey said, "Now we're getting somewhere. Let me go a step further with this. The motive in this killing has been identified as jealousy among three lesbian women, my client, another woman named Denise Rakes, and the victim, Angela Kinney."

He pauses to phrase the next question as concisely as he can. "Motive rests on Evelyn's being a female. There is a catfight over her, involving two other women. It sounds like an all-lesbian deal. But, if Evelyn did what she did in her role as a male, sort of a right brain-left brain split, where would you put your money?"

Ellis smiles. "I'm no lawyer, but in court, it might depend on how the question was put. A jury might question the whole motivation thing. If you're a man, do you kill a good-looking woman who likes you and with whom, you may be having sexual relations? That's something you and your client have to work out."

Ellis continues. "I don't think you should even get into it. For one thing, this is a military jury, not a civilian one.

They tend to think differently, especially when it comes to stuff like gays and lesbians. I doubt you can sell the argument that Evelyn is really a man and that she's really in court because she wants to protect her woman. The world isn't perfect. I think it was Voltaire who said the wheels of progress cannot roll forward without crushing a few innocent people. And even you have to admit that you client isn't totally innocent."

"Yeah," Bailey responds. "I know that all too well. She was there when Kinney was killed, and she played at least some part in it. What I have to do is show that she was not primarily culpable— and that isn't going to be easy."

Bailey shifts in his chair as if to get up. "Anything else I ought to know?"

Ellis ponders a few seconds. "Not that relates specifically to this woman. But I can give you a generalization about people in her situation. A significant proportion of them become homosexual, like your client, or bisexual without understanding why."

He stares at Bailey for a moment. "What you probably don't want to hear is that this experience, undergoing something without understanding it, typically results in a great deal of anger, When the anger and frustration mount up enough, a common way out is suicide or sometimes violence directed at others. You could be dealing with that here, I don't know."

"That's the trouble," Bailey says. "I don't, either."

Bailey stands up. "But at least I know a helluva lot more than I did before I came in here. And I think I understand my client a lot better."

Bailey reaches across the desk to shake Ellis' hand. "Bob, I can't tell you how much I appreciate your help. Any time you need some free legal advice, you know where to come. And I mean that."

Getting up, Ellis chuckles. "Well, I hope that if I do, it won't be as complicated as this one."

Bailey takes his leave, wondering how, if at all, he can use his new-found information and understanding on Evelyn's behalf.

An hour later, Bailey calls St. Joseph's Hospital in Omaha, Nebraska. In the course of the call, he learns something that he was not looking for: Cecilia Riley is dying of cervical cancer. She has just been sent home for terminal care.

WHITE SANDS MISSILE RANGE 22 OCTOBER 1983

Colonel Denison had been assigned to Evelyn's case from his usual duty station at Fort Carson, Colorado and for the duration of the trial is given an office belonging to an officer on extended leave.

This morning, seated at his borrowed desk in his borrowed office, his "chambers", he confronts an unprecedented situation. With him to try to sort it out are all the principals in the court-martial, minus the jurors and Evelyn.

"You're asking me," he tells Bailey, "to halt these proceedings at this point so that an accused murderer can just go off on a trip to Omaha?"

"Yes, sir," Bailey responds. "That's right as far as it goes. But it's not just a trip to Omaha."

He clears his throat and sits up straighter on his chair. "My client's mother is dying of cancer. She isn't expected to live more than a couple of days."

"I know that," Denison gesturing toward the papers on his desk. "I have the application for compassionate leave right here. But you have to concede, Captain, that this is a highly unusual request at a most inopportune time. How long has your client known about this?"

"She was just informed last night. Apparently, her mother wanted to slip away quietly and not burden her daughter with this while she's going through the trial."

Denison concedes that he could see the point, but adds that it does not make the situation any easier to handle.

Bailey continues. "Sir, I made a quick search and couldn't find any precedents that might govern the granting of compassionate leave to a defendant on trial. There might be some, but you understand that by the time I find them and the court studies them and makes its ruling, it probably will be too late."

He clears his throat and adds an emotional appeal. "Your Honor, I happen to know that Mrs. Riley, the defendant's mother, is virtually the only person in the world who is really close to my client. They have an unusually strong bond, and I'm afraid that if Specialist Davis is not allowed to see her mother in her last hours, she will be affected to the point at which she might not be able to assist in her own defense."

"Captain Bailey, I don't even know if compassionate leave is in the picture here. As I understand Army policy, it has to be granted by the individual's commanding officer, and I have no idea who that might be."

"Sir, Specialist Davis is in the unusual position right now of not really having a commanding officer. When she was remanded to the jurisdiction of this court, she was detached permanently from her unit here. Technically, you'd have to go all the way up to the post commander to find someone who might be defined as her CO."

Denison doesn't want to hear this. "I'm not about to drag the post commander into this. Captain, what else do you have?"

"Well, sir," Bailey said, "officially, my client has been delivered into the custody of the provost marshal pending the outcome of this trial. That would be Colonel Silverstine."

"Has Colonel Silverstine been consulted?"

This gives Bailey a chance to play his trump. "Yes sir! As a matter of fact, I have a disposition form signed by the colonel."

He takes a green sheet of paper out of his briefcase and hands it to Denison.

The judge scans the form, frowning. "According to this, the defendant has the approval of the officer responsible for her custody to leave this post and travel to Omaha, Nebraska for not longer than seven days."

"That's correct, sir," Bailey said." And as you can see, the provost marshal has left the logistics of her trip to the discretion of her defense attorney, me, and makes me responsible for her return."

Denison slips the disposition form into the growing file of documents related to the court-martial and looks to Captain Mike Larson. "The prosecution has been silent. Do you have anything to say about this, one way or another?"

"Your Honor," Larson says, "the Army recognizes, as you do, that this matter is highly irregular and calls for the exercise of a great deal of leeway on the part of the court. We have no strong objections to recessing the trial for a week, or however long it takes short of a week. We are at a point in presenting evidence where an interruption would not be detrimental to the case, and we would accede to the defendant's request."

He pauses and looks at Bailey. "We have only one request: that the jurors not be informed of the cause of the recess. Will you agree to that?"

Bailey hastily agrees. He knows that Larson will be concerned about the effect on the jurors' sympathy if they know that Evelyn has been excused to visit the bedside of her dying mother.

"We're fine with that, sir," he tells the judge, "and I can personally guarantee that the defendant will be back in court at the appointed time. She was released in my custody once before, during pre-trial investigation, and no problems resulted."

"All right. You go ahead and make the arrangements with the M.P.s and Colonel Silverstine and whoever else you have to deal with. I'll recess the court for one week, and tell the jurors the break is for administrative matters. Anything further?"

Bailey and the others shake their heads, stand and salute.

OMAHA, NEBRASKA
23 OCTOBER 1983

On the flight from El Paso to Omaha, with a change of planes in Denver, Evelyn sits in a center seat in coach class, between Pat Bailey and a black female M.P. sergeant named Ruth Devon. All are wearing their green Class A uniforms. Sergeant Devon is unidentifiable as a military policewoman save for the crossed-pistol insignia on her lapel. She is without a sidearm or the M.P. armband.

"That was the way Colonel Silverstine has decreed it. Specialist Davis is going to see her terminally ill mother," Bailey tells Sergeant Devon. "For her sake and especially the Army's, she's going to look like just another soldier, traveling with two companions in uniform. I don't know what the book says, and, this time, I don't care. As far as I'm concerned, she's not a prisoner or defendant until she gets back here."

Bailey had thanked Silverstine for his consideration, wondering to himself what had come over the straight-arrow colonel. He has a glimmering suspicion that Silverstine is having second thoughts about the Army's and El Paso P.D.'s handling of the case.

When the plane lands in Omaha, Bailey picks up the rental car he has arranged from White Sands. The three of them drive to Cecilia Riley's home.

"You go on in," he tells Evelyn, "We'll wait out here for a little while. If anybody asks who we are, just tell 'em we're friends who came to be with you. And if you aren't out in an hour or so, we're going on to the motel."

He hands Evelyn a slip of paper with the motel's phone number. "Just call and we'll come and pick you up, and play it from there."

Sergeant Devon protests, but to no avail.

"We're an escort, Sergeant, not a guard detail. Specialist Davis isn't going anywhere, and we're not going to clutter things up." He gestures for Evelyn to go on to the house,

Uncertain as to what she will find, and fearing the worst, Evelyn enters her mother's home. An elderly woman from the Church of the Living God is sitting in the living room, watching television with the sound turn low.

"How's Mama?" Evelyn asks.

"Not so good child," the woman answers. "We've been taking turns watching over her, but there isn't anything more we can do — or the doctors, either. You'd better go on up; I don't think there's much time."

Evelyn goes upstairs and opens the door to her mother's room. It's dark and musty. An IV pole is next to the bed stand on which are numerous medicine containers.

"I've been waiting for you," Cecilia says in a weak, hoarse voice. "I didn't want you to come, but in my heart I knew you would."

Cecilia is a gaunt ghost. She weighs just over a hundred pounds. Most of her hair has fallen out.

Evelyn sits on the edge of her bed and takes her mother's hand in both of hers. "Mama, why didn't you tell me? I would have come sooner."

Cecilia tries to smile. "I know, baby. But there isn't anything you could have done, and you have enough cares already."

Evelyn had written to her mother nearly every day after her arrest. She realizes now that in her letters she has been doing the same thing as Cecilia — trying to spare her mother's feelings by not revealing the full scope of the trouble she is in. "I understand, Mama. I wish I had known sooner, but Lord willing .... ."

Cecilia interrupts. "I've told the boys, and now I'm telling you. When I go, I want to be buried from the funeral home, not the church."

Evelyn almost gasps. "But Mama, the church has meant everything to you. Why?"

"Some of them deserted my child. They know about it."

Cecilia tells of hearing talk among the church members about the abomination Evie was involved in. One church member had said within earshot of Cecilia that Evelyn should never be allowed to ever show her face in the church.

"Mama, you can't let what they think about me keep you from having your funeral at the church. It's the place you love."

"Don't you fret about that Evie. There isn't time for that. It is time for me to die and I'm not afraid to. I have tried to live by God's rules. I have loved you, no matter what. I am not the one to judge you. I never have and I'm not about to start now."

Evelyn can't reply. She just squeezes her mother's hand harder. She is reaching her bottom. She has caused her mother so much pain in her final days at the church. She says to herself, "*You're worthless. It would have been better if you died at birth. You're a freak that no one but Denise has ever truly accepted.*"

Cecilia's eyes close, but she opens them again. "It's Christmas, baby."

Evelyn wonders if her mother is slipping into delusion. "Look under the bed. There's an early Christmas present there."

Evelyn kneels down and pulls an unwrapped rectangular box from under the bed.

"Go ahead, open it up."

The box contains a pair of matching white T-shirts. On the front of one is printed HIS. The other reads HER's.

"One of these is yours," Cecilia said. "You will keep the one that belongs to you and, with God's help, find someone who will accept the other. You've been my little girl all these years and you still are, but I can accept you as a man if that's what's in your soul. Anyone who doesn't, well — you just don't have to deal with them."

Cecilia appears to doze off again for a second, but awakes to continue. "You'll see there's a bible in that box, too. It was mine; now it's yours. Whenever you read it, you'll know I'm there. Pray for God's guidance. You might not understand His ways, but He has a plan for you."

Cecilia coughs a deep, racking sound. "If there's to be any changing, God will do it for you."

She closes her eyes again. This time Evelyn can see that she is asleep.

Evelyn is now Evie without realizing it. She takes off her uniform jacket and shoes and curls up in the old easy chair beside her mother's bed. Soon, in the deep silence of the darkened room, she, too, drifts off to sleep.

Something, not a sound but a feeling, startles Evelyn into wakefulness. She looks at her watch and realizes she had been asleep for nearly an hour.

She gets up from the chair and again sits on the edge of her mother's bed, saying softly, "Mama, can you hear me? Do you want to wake up?"

There is no reply. Fearing what she may find, Evelyn feels for a pulse in Cecilia's throat.

Throwing herself on the bed. Evelyn hugs her mother's body and cries as if she is a little girl again, hurt by another of life's jagged edges. She is now spiritually a motherless child. The only other person who had never judged her is gone.

When she is out of tears, she sits up. She folds Cecilia's hands across her sunken chest and straightens out the bedclothes. Then she puts her shoes and jacket back on. Leaning over Cecilia, she whispers, "Goodbye, Mama. I love you so much."

Evelyn goes downstairs where the churchwoman still sits in front of the TV. "She's gone," Evelyn said to the woman. "I have a call to make. Please call the church and ask the reverend to come and bless her. Then I want you to call the funeral home and say she's ready."

Evelyn picks up the phone. "Captain, this is Evelyn Davis. There's nothing more to do here. Mama's gone, and I got to say goodbye to her. Nobody wants me around here. I'm ready to go back."

WHITE SANDS MISSILE RANGE
25 OCTOBER 1983

On the trip back from Omaha, Bailey wants in the worst way to find something to say to his client that, not only would ease the burden of her grief, but penetrate the wall of relative isolation behind which she has chosen to reside in. He and the woman M.P. awarkwardly extend their condolences.

She doesn't speak a word all the way back to White Sands, not even when she is led back into the M.P. station to be locked up for the night. Her eyes say that she is now ready for God to finish his work.

Bailey has had little personal experience with emotional isolation, depression and despair, but he knows it when he sees it. He asks the M.P.s on night duty to quietly keep an eye on Evelyn. "Not a real suicide watch. Just be aware. Okay?"

WHITE SANDS COURTROOM
26 OCTOBER 1983

A degree of this concern appears to be shared by the military judge. In a brief conference before the court-martial resumed, Colonel Denison quizzes Bailey about the defendant's readiness to proceed.

"Captain, your client has been through what would be a traumatic experience for anyone under any circumstances. We can go ahead without reference to her personal feelings, but I'd rather not if there is any substantive question as to her ability to participate in her defense. What do you think?"

"I would entertain a motion for a continuance if you believe it is warranted."

Bailey thanks the judge for his consideration, but he states that, while a delay may be useful, in fact, it may be harder on Evelyn than going ahead with the trial.

"Sir, I don't think any purpose would be served by letting that girl sit alone in her cell any further with her grief and loneliness. Besides, she's a good soldier; she knows what her duty is, and I think she's ready to go ahead with it."

Denison turns to Larson and Walters, the prosecution team. "Does the government have any input on this?"

"Not really, sir. Captain Bailey is in the best position to know his client's state of readiness for trial. We would have only one concern — that her emotional state might be so apparent, so visible, as to evoke prejudicial sympathy in the jurors, or even undue curiosity on their part that could be a distraction."

Bailey shakes his head. "To all outward appearances she seems to be well enough put together. I saw her briefly this morning. She was cleaned up and dressed up in a military manner. She isn't saying anything to me or anybody else but that's not unusual. I don't think the jury will see anything in her demeanor or behavior that is inconsistent with a person facing a capital charge."

"All right, then," the judge says. "Let's go."

When the court reconvenes a few minutes later, Denison takes a minute to address the jury.

"On behalf of the Army, I want to apologize for any inconvenience this unexpected recess may have caused you. A non-evidentiary matter came up that we had to dispose of before we could go on. That having been accomplished, we are ready to resume."

"Do any of the jurors have any questions?" With no one responding, the colonel gestures toward Larson, "The Army may call its next witness."

Leopoldo Armijo, an FBI agent working out of Las Cruses, produces and describes various items of physical evidence the government had removed from Denise Rakes' house. These include items of clothing, a bed sheet, a white nylon cord, a yellow electric extension cord — both with reddish brown stains — two rugs, a sample of human hair and two sets of nylon fibers, brown and green.

Armijo states that all the items had been sent to the FBI laboratory in Washington for forensic examination. "The brown nylon fibers, which were taken from the sheet and a pair of sweat pants in Rakes' house and from

Angela Kinney's body, matched one of the rugs. Green fibers found on the sheet and on the victim matched those from the other rug. Grouping tests on a blood sample taken from the victim's body matched the blood stains on the rope. The human hair fragments were not suitable for significant microscopic examination."

Bailey cross-examines the FBI agent briefly, asking him only to provide additional details about the location of the blood stains on the rope. The attorney recognizes that the forensic evidence establishes only that Angela Kinney had been in Denise Rakes' house and suggests only that she had been strangled with the rope or extension cord, or both.

None of it linked Evelyn Davis directly to the killing, a fact which Bailey hopes the jury would see as supporting his opening assertion that the government has no concrete evidence against his client.

The agent is excused. Then Larson speaks the words Bailey has been preparing for since the day he was assigned the case:

"The government calls Denise Rakes."

Bailey is correct in his prediction that Larson will have Rakes decked out as the poster girl for Credible Witnesses. As she walks from the back of the courtroom to the witness stand, Bailey notes her clothing - navy blue skirt, white blouse, red scarf, medium-heeled pumps: her demeanor confident, business-like.

Larson's suggestions relative to presenting a demure appearance couldn't overcome Rakes' natural attributes. As she turns to stand in front of the witness chair, there was a noticeable stir among the small audience. Bailey images that she could wear a Mother Hubbard and combat boots and she would still be a hot item. He wonders if her lush figure and delicate coffee-colored face will work better for the prosecution or for the defense.

Rakes is sworn in and settles into the witness chair, back straight, legs together, hands clasped loosely in her lap. She looks at no one in the room except Larson as he approaches her and begins his examination.

After eliciting her full name, Denise Louise Rakes, the prosecutor takes her through the routine of identification: residence, El Paso, but formerly of 413 Vanguard Street, White Sands Missile Range; age, 27; married to a soldier named Vance, stationed in Korea; one child, a boy.

Then Larson starts building his foundation.

"Do you know the accused in this case?"

"Yes, I do."

"And is she in the courtroom today?"

"Yes".

"And her name is?"

"Well, Bandit - Evelyn Davis."

For the first time, Denise Rakes glances at Evelyn. Evelyn looks back, impassive.

Larson turns to Colonel Denison,

"Your Honor, for the purpose of keeping these identifications straight, I'd like the record to show that references to Bandit or Bandit Riley are references to the accused, Evelyn Davis."

Denison nods to the stenographic reporter. "Without objection, let that clarification be inserted in the record at this point."

Larson resumes.

"Okay. How did you first meet Evelyn Davis?"

"I had an open house for New Year's and she came over."

"Did you begin to frequently associate with the accused after that?"

"Yes. After that point my husband left for Korea — that was January 7th — and from then on, whenever I would have time, she and I would spend time."

"How much time did you have?"

Rakes explains that she works a 40-hour week at a bank branch on the post and another 20 to 25 hours a week at the Officers' Club. She also uses her husband's sound system and record-playing equipment to host disco sessions at the White Sands NCO Club.

"In your association with the accused, did you ever meet an Angela Kinney?"

"Yes."

"When did you first meet her?"

"I formally met her on April 7th. Bandit brought her over to my house."

Rakes states that, though she had seen Kinney before the visit to her house on April 7th, Evelyn had never introduced Angela to her. She describes a night at Whispers when Evelyn elected to stay at the bar with Kinney while Denise went home by herself and an encounter with Kinney at Evelyn's quarters.

Rakes testifies further as to her relationship with Evelyn. "Now, did you and Specialist Davis, the accused, have a relationship other than just going out?"

"Oh, yes, we—a couple of times. Yes, we slept together, but it was not that we were lovers or anything like that."

With this, and with Larson's subsequent questioning of Rakes about her activities with Evelyn, Bailey detects what may be a pattern. The prosecutor appears to be establishing, mostly by indirection, that, as the relationship between the two women developed, Evelyn was the more aggressive pursuer and Rakes the pursued.

Larson moves on to the night of April 7th, 1983, the night Angela Kinney died. Rakes testifies that she was napping in her apartment at 413 Vanguard when her phone rang. By the time she went to answer it, it had stopped ringing.

"And did anything of note happen after that?"

"Well, the doorbell rang. And I went to the door and it was Bandit and she had Angela with her. When they came in, Bandit said 'I want you to meet my friend Angela, she's from Fort Bliss', and I said okay."

"And what did you do?"

"I went into the bathroom to change. I think I had my robe on at the time, and I put on a pair of jeans and a sweater."

"How did your meeting with Angela Kinney go?"

"Well, when I walked back in they were sitting on the couch, and Kinney looked at me and said, 'Bandit gave me your message' or something like that "

"What was your reaction to that?"

"I just kind of flung it off. I knew right then it was something's cooking here."

"Did she describe to you the things that the accused had allegedly said about you?"

"She said something to the effect that, 'You had your chance. Now Bandit and I are together.' "

121

"What was your understanding of that statement?"

"Just that Specialist Davis was playing some sort of game."

"What happened after that?"

"They were sitting on my loveseat. Bandit reached around and put her arm around Angela. Then Bandit grabbed her throat with her right hand and started choking her."

"What, if anything, was said at this time?"

"Bandit said, like, 'Angela, you really don't know me. I've been telling you ever since I met you, that I am a Satanist'."

"And she was! She was really choking her." I said, "Bandit, let her go, please, just let her go, I don't know what the problem is."

"Did the accused's actions surprise you?"

"Oh, yeah. Without a doubt. You know, getting over to my place and choking her because she said something to me that Bandit didn't like. It was like—like it was all preplanned."

Rakes tells the court that this display of jealousy and possessiveness on Bandit's part was unexpected, because she had told Bandit that the two of them could never have a long-term committed relationship. Although she had affairs with other women, she would never leave her husband.

Larson presses on. "Now, what happened after the incident where the accused began to choke Specialist Kinney?"

I said, "Okay, Bandit let her go and I got up, and walked out of the room. When I came back they had gone into the living room, only a couple of steps away.

They were fighting. Bandit hit her in the face and they were tussling. It was like Angela tried to run for the door."

"Were they exchanging blows?"

"Like I said, Specialist Davis hit her in the face. She, in turn, kicked Specialist Davis where it counts."

"Who had the advantage?"

"No doubt, Bandit."

"While they were struggling at the door and Angela Kinney was trying to get out, what, if anything, did you do?"

"I said something like, "Why don't you guys take this elsewhere, okay?""

"What was the response?"

"Bandit tells Angela, 'The only reason I'm not kicking your ass is because Denise has real nice furniture'."

Bailey's head drops in a gesture of disbelief.

"Did Angela manage to get out the door and escape?"

"No, she didn't try after that. She told Bandit, "Okay, that's fine, just let me go and we can talk about it.""

"So they did stop?"

"Oh, yeah, they were holding a conversation."

"What happened after that?"

"Bandit was talking again about how she was a Satanist. She told Angela that I had gone through some of it, too: that I wanted to be one and was willing to go through the training or whatever. Then, they went on talking about Satanism. Angela was saying something like she wouldn't have any problems with it."

"Didn't this surprise you, that one minute Angela and the accused were fighting. And the next minute they were talking about Satanism?"

"I don't remember the extent of the conversation, but they both seemed to have calmed down some."

"What happened after this conversation?"

"Bandit looks at me and says, 'Well, go get a rope. I said I didn't have one, and she said twine or something like that would do."

"You didn't know what she wanted a rope for?"

"No".

"Okay. Go ahead."

"So I walked out to my garage and got an extension cord, and when I came back Bandit said, "Now I want you to tie her up."

"Go ahead."

"So I asked why Bandit wanted me to tie her up. She looked at me and said, "I'd just as soon kill you, too." By this time my hands were shaking."

"What was Angela Kinney doing?"

"She was sitting there. She said, "Okay, fine, if Denise can do it, I can do it, too."

"She could do what?"

"She was saying that if I could do this Satanism stuff with Bandit, she would try it, too."

"What did you do then?"

"I started wrapping the cord around her legs and it was just loose, because it's a real thick cord. Bandit pushed me out of the way and said, "Just get out of the way, I'll do it myself."

"You say Angela Kinney was sitting. Where was she sitting?"

"On the floor. She stuck out her hands and her legs and in some manner told you to go ahead and tie me up?

Yeah. So when Bandit pushed me out of the way, she wrapped the cord around her hands, and there was a piece of white twine on the end of the cord, and she wrapped that around her neck."

"What was your reaction to this?"

"I said," What are you doing?" Bandit said, "Nothing."

"What did Angela Kinney do?"

"She looked up and said, 'Bandit, are you going to hurt me?' So Bandit says, 'Oh, no, I'm not going to do anything to you.'"

"And how did Angela respond to that?"

"She said, 'Okay'."

"So now Angela had one cord around her ankles, one around her arms, and the other cord, or piece of twine, around her neck?"

"That's right."

"And then what happened?"

"Well, Bandit looked down at her and said, 'Angela, you're a fool. I'd never let anybody put a rope around my neck.' And then she just started to pull."

"How do you mean that?"

"Bandit's hands were crossed, with one end of the cord in each one. And when she started to pull, the cord started to tighten."

"Around Kinney's neck?"

"Yes. Angela was struggling. So I went over to where they were and Bandit and I started tussling. I got my hand between the cord and Angela's neck, and I started trying to pull it loose, I could hear her breathing, and she was trying to get air. Then, Bandit knocked me out of the way. I kinda hit my head falling against a chair. When I got up Angela was lying on the floor, but... "

"Was the rope still around her neck?"

"Yes. And Bandit still had hold of it."

"Then what happened?"

"Bandit got up and I saw she had a switchblade in her hand. She looked at me and said, 'I'm going to cut her up. That's what we do, you know, that's our thing; we like blood'."

"What did you do?"

"I said, "Oh, God, you can't do this". But she said, 'Well, I've got to draw some blood.' She took the switchblade and kinda cut her on the neck - nicked her or whatever."

"Did Angela Kinney react when she was cut?"

"No, she was just laying there. There was no movement, no nothing, she was just laying there."

Then, Rakes testifies that Bandit told her to go find something to put the body in. At this point, she was so distraught that she lost control of her bladder and wet herself. She went to a linen closet and found a sheet. Bandit threw it aside and went to the adjoining room and returned with Rakes' husband's Army poncho. She then laid it on the floor and kinda rolled the body onto it."

"Then what?"

"Bandit told me to go get my car to put the body in. I told her I was almost out of gas, so she said, to move it and she would pull her car in. She did that. She backed her car up where mine had been parked.

"What, if anything, did she say during this?"

"She said, 'Well, are you going to help me or what?'
She said if I didn't help her, she'd just leave and they'd find
Angela's body in my house and think I'd killed her."

"And did you help her or call the M.P.s?"

"I didn't know. I was afraid."

"Okay. Go ahead with what happened next."

"Well, together we drug the body out through the
garage and put it in Bandit's car. It was a hatchback, and
we just kinda lifted it in. She said she was going to go get
Angela's car. She said she'd put Angela in it. We drove
over to Angela's house to get her car. When we got there
Bandit told me to go in and put on some dry shoes while
she put Angela in her car. When she was finished she
came into the house and got me and we left."

"Go on."

"Well, Bandit said she would drive Angela's car and I
should drive hers. She told me to drive ahead of her in case
there were any M.P.s or something. We drove towards
El Paso. I was in front and she was behind me and we
were driving like 15 miles an hour. The M.P.s waved us
through. We hadn't even got to the sign that says 'You
are leaving White Sands Missile Range' before I looked
back and saw that Bandit was slowing down. There was
an M.P. car behind her with its lights flashing."

"What did you do?"

"After she slowed down and pulled over to the side,
I just kept driving toward El Paso. I drove into the first
apartment complex I came to in El Paso and just waited
as close to the road as I could get so she'd see me. A few
minutes later she came down the road and pulled into
where I was parked. She said the M.P.s had pulled her
over because they thought she was driving too slow or

something and might have been drinking. She said she convinced them she was okay and they let her go."

"Then what did you do?"

"Well, she got out of Angela's car and got in with me in her car, because from that point, I just refused to drive. My hands were shaking. We drove away and headed back toward White Sands. Every once in a while she'd slow down and look around as if she was looking for something. She turned off the road and onto a road that led by the power plant."

"What were you doing through all this?"

"At this point I was just sitting there crying. Bandit looked at me and said. "I don't want you to nut up on me now. It's too late for that".

"She got the body out of the back of the car. I don't know what she did with it. I was just sitting there crying. Then we drove back to White Sands. She drove Angela's car and I drove hers. We went back to my house and cleaned it up. She put everything there that looked like evidence in a garbage bag. She said she'd take it with her and get rid of it at work the next day. Bandit stayed at my house that night."

"Did you both go to work the next day?"

"Yes."

"Now, if I may, let's move ahead to the night of April 10th at the White Sands Officers' Club. You were there with the accused?"

"Yes, we were both there, but we weren't together."

"Tell the court generally what happened."

"Well, Bandit came over to where I was sitting and said she knew that I had just bought a drink for another girl named Sabrina and she accused me of trying to pick Sabrina up."

"What was her attitude or demeanor at this time?"

"Mad and jealous."

"Then what happened?"

"Later on I went to the women's restroom and Bandit and Sabrina were both there."

"Did you have a conversation at that point?"

"Yes, I asked Sabrina what she was doing saying I had bought her a drink. She said a waitress had told her that Bandit had bought her the drink."

"What was Bandit's response to that?"

"She denied it. Then Sabrina and I started arguing, and then fighting. She hit me and we just went at it. Some of the other women in there broke it up, and we went our ways".

Rakes tells of being questioned by the El Paso police, with Army investigators looking on. She says that she was allowed to call an attorney, who advised her not to make a statement. But the questioning continued. At one point, one of the officers told her that, while Evelyn was being interrogated, she said Rakes had killed Angela.

"How did you respond to that?"

"By then, they're telling me that I'm going to be put to death, you know, that's she's blaming me for all of this. So I just said, 'Hey, I'll tell you what happened. I was wrong for not coming up front, for not saying anything. I'll tell you what happened.' And that's what I did."

Larson hands Rakes a document and asks if it is a copy of the statement she made that night. She confirms that it is. Larson had previously had it admitted into evidence.

"Just a few more questions. Now, at first you refused to talk to the investigating officers in this case. Is that correct?"

"Yes."

"And why is that?"

"I was advised by my attorney not to."

"And you're testifying here today because of what reason?"

"My lawyer went through the Army to get immunity for this."

"Mrs. Rakes, I have only one other question for you. On the night of her death, when you left your quarters was there any doubt in your mind that Angela Collette Kinney was dead?"

"There was no doubt in my mind about it at all."

Larson states he has no further questions and Rakes temporarily leaves the witness stand.

The court-martial takes a brief recess for a quick lunch before Patrick Bailey begins his cross-examination of Denise Rakes. His client has sat impassively through Rakes's direct testimony; yet he senses the vibrations within Evelyn as the woman she loves accuses her of murder.

Colonel Denison asks Bailey if the defense is ready to cross-examine. Captain Bailey replies that, with the court's permission, he will begin the next morning. There are no objections.

As the judge leaves his bench and the room clears, Bailey turns to Evelyn. "I want you to know", he says, "that you handled yourself perfectly today. You listened quietly. You didn't make faces or squirm around. I know it was hard to listen to when you know the real story.

Tonight try the best you can to put this on the back shelf."

He puts a hand on Evelyn's shoulder. "Remember, that was just her side of it. Tomorrow I'm gonna start shooting big holes in it. You'll be able to get up there when it's your turn and we'll let the jury make a comparison between your testimony and hers. I think they'll get the message."

Evelyn's eyes avoid meeting Bailey's.

That night in her cell is the worst of her young life. She faces death or prison if convicted. The woman she is willing to die to protect is trying to have the Army put her to death. Her mother is gone, and the only person on her side is a young white Army lawyer who seems all too relaxed.

White Sands Courtroom
26 October 1983

When the court reconvenes in the morning, Evelyn Davis seems different to Patrick Bailey. Her body language and inner demeanor signal to him surrender. He guesses that, in some way, she has come to terms with her betrayal by Denise Rakes and is prepared to accept whatever comes next.

Bailey's cross-examination of Rakes begins.

"Let's see, Mrs. Rakes, why don't we start out with a statement that's been admitted into evidence. That statement accurately reflects what you told your questioners at the time?"

"Yes. Since that time, I have been able to think what happened: little details that I didn't give then; but I was under a lot of pressure at the time."

"I can understand that. You didn't lie to them, though, did you?"

"No, sir, I did not."

"And you're here under a grant of testimonial immunity."

"Yes, sir."

"And that means that what you say in this courtroom cannot be used against you at a further proceeding, is that correct? Is that your understanding?"

"As far as the military is concerned, yes, sir. Yes, that is correct."

"And isn't it also correct that you still could be prosecuted for murder if some jurisdiction wanted to?"

"Yes sir."

"And would it be probable that somebody might look at your testimony here and decide whether or not to prosecute you? Wouldn't that make sense?"

"I don't know, sir."

Bailey hopes this exchange will be enough to plant the idea with the jurors that Rakes' court-martial testimony will, of necessity, be given so that a civilian jury later on may not find anything in it with which to convict her. He moves on.

"Do you know a lady named Cindy Eller?"

"Yes, I do."

"Isn't it a fact that she lived with you for some time in your home with your husband?"

"No sir."

"And if she said that, that would be a lie?"

"Yes sir, it would be."

"And if other people came in and said that, that would be a lie?"

"Yes sir, it would."

Bailey goes on to establish the lesbian relationship between Rakes and Cindy Eller.

Rakes asserts that she was not in love with Eller and denies that she ever said she would divorce her husband and live with her in a permanent relationship.

Then Bailey moves on to the night of the "catfight" at the NCO Club.

"Isn't it a fact Mrs. Rakes that you got into that fight with Sabrina James because you were the one who was jealous? Didn't you think that she was trying to get the attentions of Specialist Davis?"

"No sir."

"Isn't it true that you made comments to the effect of 'stay away from my woman'?"

"No sir."

"And if you were heard to say those things — that wouldn't be a true statement if someone came in and said they heard that from you?"

"No sir, it would not be true."

"Isn't it a fact that you made statements to the effect of 'I'm going to mess up your pretty face, stay away from my woman'?"

"No sir"

"Now, do you know a woman by the name of Johnnie Jenson?"

"Yes sir, I do."

"Did you hear that she was going to appear in this case as a defense witness?"

"No sir. I think I've spoken to her once since I left White Sands. She called while I was in El Paso to visit and I wasn't there. But I have not seen or spoken to her at all, other than that one time."

"Well, isn't it true that you called her about a month ago and told her that if she appeared in this case as a witness you'd kill her?"

"No sir."

"So if she came into court and testified to that effect she'd be lying?"

"Yes sir, she would."

"And Johnnie Jenson, your good friend, would be lying if she said you called her?"

"Yes sir, she would. Yes, sir, she would. I have not been in contact with her."

"Do you remember getting into fist fights with Cindy Eller?"

"No sir."

"You don't remember an incident wherein you were angry with both your husband and Cindy and you ended up breaking a wine glass and threatening her with it and then, yourself, getting cut on the forehead?"

"No sir. That didn't happen either."

"And again, if Cindy Eller testified to that effect, she'd be lying?"

"Yes sir."

Rakes is becoming progressively more flustered. Both feet are now on the floor. The calmness in her responses is gone. His tone of voice that has been conversational portrays anxiety.

Bailey continues. "With regard to your incident with Sabrina James, isn't it true that you ended up sitting on top of her, choking her with your hands?"

"No sir."

"That's not true?"

"She was..., we were fighting. No sir, that's not true."

"And again, if people who witnessed that fight came into court and under oath would testify that that's what you did, they would all be lying?"

"Yes sir."

Bailey continues in this vein for a few more questions, giving Rakes the chance to swear that anyone who testified in contradiction of her story would be lying.

He relinquishes the witness; but the examination of Rakes isn't quite over. The judge has questions for her. He takes Rakes through some of her previous testimony. "From the time you realized that Specialist Davis was trying to harm Angela Kinney, did you do anything to help Specialist Davis?"

"No sir. Not at all."

"You also testified that after Angela Kinney was dead you drove the car off-post and drove her various places while the body was being disposed of. Were you helping her or aiding her in disposing of the body?"

"No sir."

"Why were you doing what you were doing?"

"I was afraid. I didn't know what to do."

"What were you afraid of?"

"That she would leave the body at my house, you know, just go out and say that I killed her. I believe that was the sole purpose for bringing her to my house."

Bailey thinks to himself, *'Thanks, Your Honor. I couldn't have done better myself. You just painted her even farther into the corner.'*

Members of the jury have the option of questioning witnesses themselves, sending their queries through the judge. But none have anything to ask Rakes. For Bailey, this is a good sign, indicating that he has raised enough questions with Rakes that the jurors don't feel the need to pursue it further. His big problem is seated next to him. *'Will she fight for her life?'* Given the level of betrayal, Bailey prepares for the worst.

The prosecution and Bailey are finished with Rakes. She is dismissed as a witness.

The court takes a brief recess before Larson concludes his presentation of evidence.

As they sit at the defense table, Bailey asks Evelyn how she thinks he has done with Denise Rakes.

"All right, I guess, but ..." she doesn't finish the sentence. The words just seem to hang without direction. They do little to lessen Bailey's growing concern.

Attempting to reverse what seems to be a growing tide of self-destruction, Bailey says, "We haven't even really gotten started yet. What we have done is plant some seeds today that may grow into some really big, ugly weeds before this is over."

He pauses, and then asks Evelyn: "After hearing what she said on the stand, do you still think you have to protect her? Is this the kind of person you feel obligated to?"

Evelyn doesn't answer. Her gaze is fixed on the hands tightly clasped in her lap.

Bailey anticipates that his client may state her innocence, but accept the guilt for both.

After the recess, Larson calls a few more witnesses to wrap up his case. They are mostly civilian policemen from El Paso or M.P.s, contributing or confirming details of the investigation, details which, while not substantial, are essential to Larson's goal of presenting a complete picture with no holes Bailey can exploit.

The court-martial breaks for lunch.

When court reconvenes for the afternoon, Bailey makes the usual motion to dismiss the charges against Evelyn, Larson makes the usual argument against the motion and Judge Denison issues the usual denial of the motion.

Now it is Bailey's turn to call witnesses.

But first, the judge explains to the jurors that the defense testimony will be partly in person, by live witnesses, and partly through written, sworn statements submitted to Bailey and stipulated to by the prosecution.

Bailey opens reading the statement given under oath by Cindy Ann Eller who has been discharged from the Army for homosexuality

Her statement states that while stationed at White Sands she had become the lesbian lover of Denise Rakes, and had lived with Rakes and Rakes' husband in their quarters. The statement went on to say "Although Denise likes women sexually, I really don't know if she is a lesbian or not. She has a temper and used to get very upset when I didn't do the things she wanted me to do. She really does like to get her way. I found Denise to be a very jealous woman, both with other women who might make a pass at her husband and other women she thought made a pass at me or she thought I was interested in. Denise only lets you see the Denise she wants you to see; you never know what the real truth is."

Bailey pauses, ostensibly to turn a page of Eller's statement, but really to let the jury dwell for a moment on the commentary about Rakes' truthfulness. He reads on: "Denise and I had a couple of fights where she ended up hitting me. On one occasion when she was really mad about something, both her husband and I decided to leave. I was going out the door of her house when she grabbed me from behind and started punching me. She eventually grabbed a wine glass and broke it over a table. I struggled with her and she ended up getting a cut on her head from the glass."

"I really cared for Denise; but when her husband came back to White Sands, it ended."

Bailey moves from his reading position in front of the jury back to the counsel table. No one in the room notices him wink at Evelyn as he puts down Eller's statement and picks up the one he will use next.

No response. Evelyn continues to sit impassively.

Bailey takes up his post at a distance from the jurors and begins reading a statement given by Specialist 4 Georgiana Persons, who is stationed at White Sands and had witnessed the 'catfight' at the NCO Club.

"When I entered the restroom where the fight occurred I saw Rakes sitting on top of James, choking her. Rakes was quite angry at James. She was yelling at her to 'stay away from my woman'. After Specialist Davis and I pulled Rakes off of James, Rakes tells James that she was going to 'mess up that pretty face' and that she would kill James. She said these things. Then she grabbed a heavy glass ashtray and tried to hit James."

"James was gasping for air. Her face was scratched and bleeding. It is my impression that Rakes was really trying to hurt James."

Bailey calls his next witness, Sabrina James, the other participant in the "catfight".

She tells of Evelyn buying her a drink at the NCO Club and of Rakes threatening her and warning her to stay away from Evelyn. Then she gives her account of what happened in the restroom.

"She started choking me and she kept choking me. I thought I was going to die."

In response to Bailey's question, James relates that she was lying on the floor with Rakes on top, straddling her. "I felt the spit running out of my mouth. I couldn't swallow."

Bailey introduces two defense exhibits: photographs of James taken after the fight, showing lacerations and scratches on her face.

For his last presentation of evidence for the afternoon, Bailey introduces a statement by Specialist 4 Dan Edmonds, who had also witnessed the incident in the restroom,

"I was standing outside the door and as the door opened and closed I was able to see a portion of the fight. Ms. Rakes was yelling at Specialist 4 James, telling her 'stay away from my woman'. At one point Ms. Rakes told James that she would kill her. Ms. Rakes was sitting on top of James, choking her with her hands. Rakes remained on top of James, choking her, for, I guess, a minute."

Bailey is finished presenting evidence for the day and suggests adjourning till the next morning. Larson has no objection. Colonel Dennison raps his gavel. The long day is over,

Before the M.P. leads Evelyn away, Bailey pats her on the back, "Take heart. One nail after another is being driven into her story. Tomorrow, we'll do it again."

If she has anything to say, Evelyn doesn't.

WHITE SANDS COURTROOM
26 OCTOBER 1983

The first defense witness of the morning is Johnnie Elisa Jenson, "E.J.", a civilian who works at the White Sands NCO Club. E.J. is in her late twenties. Though attractive, there is nothing soft about her appearance or voice.

Bailey establishes first that Mrs. Jenson knew both Evelyn Davis and Denise Rakes: then asks: "Are you still friends with Denise Rakes?"

"No."

"Why not?"

"Cause about a month ago she called me and she threatened me."

"What did she say?"

"She said if I testified she'd kill me."

"What did you do?"

"I said a few kind words and hung up."

"And when she said. "If you testify I'm going to kill you," what was she talking about?"

"The trial, I guess."

"What sort of person is Denise Rakes?"

"Denise, she's — she lies a lot. She's a liar. She's just a liar."

"What else can you tell us about her?"

"She's a very jealous person. She could sit and talk to my husband and I wouldn't get upset; but if I sat and talked to her husband, she would get very angry."

"Your friendship terminated over this phone call?"

"Yes."

Bailey's next presentation is a brief written statement from Specialist 4 Frank Theison, who was formerly stationed at the White Sands health clinic and knew both Evelyn and Denise Rakes. He is now stationed in Germany, but had been assigned to the same unit as Evelyn during his stay at the missile range.

He states that he had been approached sexually by Rakes, and that on one occasion she offered him sexual favors if he would let her tie him up. He had the impression that Rakes was jealous of his friendship with Evelyn Davis.

When he finishes reading Theison's statement into the record with what he thinks is just enough emphasis on the soldier's assertion that Rakes had wanted to tie him up, Bailey asks the judge for a short recess so he can confer with his client.

The colonel grants the recess, and as the other participants stand and stretch, or mill around the courtroom, Bailey leans over and whispers to Evelyn,

"This next guy is going to take some time and he's going to say some things you may not want to hear."

"Like what?" Evelyn is passive.

"Like medical and psychological stuff that involves your personality and sexuality plus some things that might not make sense to you at first, but are important to your defense. Okay?"

"I guess. Who is this guy, anyway?"

"You know him," Bailey says. "He's a mental health guy at your clinic. You've talked to him about some of your problems."

WHITE SANDS COURTROOM
26 OCTOBER 1983

Denison gavels the court-martial back into session and Bailey calls his witness, Captain Mark Chapman, chief of community mental health at the White Sands Health Clinic.

Bailey knows that the prosecutor, Mike Larson, will stipulate that Chapman is an expert witness in the legal sense of the term. Chapman doesn't have to list his qualifications; nevertheless, Bailey chooses to take him through the exercise anyway, to be sure the jurors are impressed. The defense attorney has Chapman recite his educational background: degrees from John Hopkins and the University of Maryland and a long list of Army and civilian seminars, courses and workshops, and his experience as a clinical practitioner.

Then Bailey gets down to business, questioning Chapman about his work with Evelyn, both as a patient and as a co-worker at the clinic.

"How would you identify her sexual orientation?"

"Her sexual orientation can best be described as a transsexual. One of the hallmarks is that the person feels that they are of the opposite sex but trapped in the body of their current sex. In Specialist Davis's case, she grew up believing she was a boy. She looks at things in a masculine way, and therefore, in terms of her sexual object choice, will look towards other women because she feels very masculine."

"What makes you reach this conclusion?"

"Well, I think probably the strongest evidence is the clinical picture that she presents based on her interviews and her history, in that she's pretty much a textbook case."

Bailey goes on to ask Chapman if he had drawn any conclusions as to how Evelyn might respond in a stressful situation,

Chapin testifies that she probably would react passively, tending to avoid conflict by going along with what was expected of her. She also would internalize stress, producing physical symptoms: this would explain her medical history of migraine headaches.

Then Bailey takes Chapman to the core of the case. "Based on your knowledge of Specialist Davis, can you comment as to her likelihood to willingly engage in violent acts, more specifically physical violence?"

5,4,3,2

"Well, based on her history of trying to avoid confrontation, my opinion would be that she would try to avoid a confrontation or a conflict. She, more likely than not, would avoid the choice of violence. She would attempt to avoid the confrontation, flee, or kind of go along with what was expected of her. In terms of her choice of solutions, I would probably put violence down at the bottom of the list."

Here Bailey pauses for a couple of beats and looks pointedly at the jury. The members appear to be paying close attention to Chapman's testimony, some even hunch forward in their chairs, exactly the attitude Bailey wants.

He doesn't particularly want to ask the next question, but he figures that if he doesn't, Larson will on cross-examination. It is better to present touchy evidence upfront than to let the prosecution do it. "Did she tell you about the incident with her first husband?"

"Yes, she did."

"And that was a case where violence was used?"

"Yes."

"In fact, she didn't she tell you that she shot him?"

"That's correct."

Bailey notes some jurors shifting in their chairs.

He asks Chapman to describe the incident as Evelyn had described it to him.

"Her husband had been physically abusive. On the occasion in question, which occurred after they had separated, he came to her home and threatened her. She left and went to her mother's house. He followed. She went back to her own home. He followed again, and pursued her to an upstairs bedroom. There, she found a handgun, and fired into the ceiling. Her husband hesitated, allowing her to run back downstairs and out to her car. She tried to drive away, but the car wouldn't start. Her husband came at her again and she fired shots over his head. When he continued to approach her, she shot and wounded him."

"So that tracks with what you've been saying that that is a last-resort type of situation where she is in fear of her life?"

"Yes."

"And, again, something that is used after all the other attempts at escape have not worked?"

"That's correct."

Inwardly, Bailey breathes a sigh of relief. The account of the shooting, rather than painting Evelyn as a reckless gunslinger has dove-tailed with Chapman's description of her as one who would rather run than fight; except as a desperate last resort.

"Is there anything about a strangulation situation that reinforces your opinion?"

"My guess is that it would not be an instantaneous incident of violence, like with a gun. You just pull the trigger and bang, it's over, or stabbing them with a knife. But something that could take fifteen, twenty, thirty seconds, a minute or something like that before the victim actually succumbs. I would say it would be very difficult for somebody who is resorting to violence only as a last resort to follow through with that, unless there was a situation of shock and they just kind of did it and weren't really aware of it."

"A person with that personality would more likely be unable to carry that out given the length of time it takes, the amount of physical force to do that, and the ability to watch a person suffer that much for a length of time."

"From what you know and can predict, can you see Specialist Davis planning something like that and carrying it out?"

"I think that would be unlikely."

Bailey's next series of questions deal with the psychologically theoretical, but he is banking on the hope that the jury can reduce theory to reality and apply the reality to individuals involved in Angela Kinney's death.

First he asks Chapman to explain what was known as an antisocial personality disorder. Chapman answers that two particular traits are characteristic—rigidity and inflexibility.

"A person with that kind of disorder would find it very difficult to learn from mistakes, would have a bad temper or explosive personality, would have trouble telling the truth, and would display a callous disregard for the needs of others."

Chapman continues. "The antisocial personality disorder is not exactly related to intelligence. In fact, many people with this personality disorder are very intelligent, socially adroit, and very clever at manipulating others."

"Good at covering their tracks, so to speak?"

"Yes."

Bailey asks Chapman if he would diagnose Evelyn as suffering from an antisocial personality disorder.

"Unlikely," he replied.

"Assuming that sort of antisocial behavior, would this be a person who might be able to strangle someone?"

"For someone who had violence high on the list of the way to solve problems, the answer is yes."

"Thank you very much, sir. No further questions."

Mike Larson has very little to ask Captain Chapman during his cross-examination, His only questions are to clear up minor points as to how Chapman has formed his opinions about Evelyn's gender identity.

On redirect examination, Bailey pursues that point further, "The physiological things you mentioned, Can you explain what those are, please, and what "physiological" means just in case anyone doesn't know?"

"Sure. Specialist Davis mother's prenatal chart identified that she had been given male hormones to avert a threatened abortion. The administration of hormones early in gestation has been shown to have effects on genital development. Specialist Davis is very flat-chested, has a rather muscular build which is more masculine than feminine, and has an enlarged clitoris, which in and of itself does not mean that one is transsexual. But those findings are consistent with a syndrome called adrenogenital syndrome which can result in the masculinizing of feminine genitalia and body type."

"So again, all this taken together fits in what I believe you called earlier the textbook case?"

"That's correct."

Chapman is dismissed as a witness. Bailey makes a mental note to the effect that he has advanced the defense's case significantly. Chapman had painted a picture of Evelyn showing that not only is she nonviolent by nature, but has an abhorrence of violence which might lead her to go to great lengths to avoid it. Bailey is pleased that through Chapman's testimony, the record will show the most salient points he had gotten from his interview with Dr. Robert Ellis.

It has been an intense morning, and the judge orders an hour's break. Bailey uses the time to reassure Evelyn.

"It might not seem like it to you," Bailey tells his client, "but we've chipping big hunks out of the Army's case against you. When Denise Rakes told her story you probably thought it was all over. But that would be true only if the jury believed her. I think they're getting more skeptical about her all the time."

When the trial resumes, Bailey calls Jackie Sanders, who had been Evelyn's lover when the two of them were stationed at Fort Mead, Maryland. She relates that she and Evelyn lived together with their respective children in a big house as if they were a family.

She testifies as to how caring and loving Evelyn had been, how hard she worked at two off-duty jobs.

"Why did she work so much?"

"She worked that hard to keep our home. Our rent was seven hundred dollars a month: food, the phone, everything; the kids, their clothes, their birthday parties and what not."

"So she was interested in taking care of her loved ones?"

"Yes."

"Is that typical in what one might see in a lesbian relationship?"

"Yes."

"The time that you knew her, did you ever hear of anything or see her in any way involved in what's commonly called Satanism?"

"No."

"Do you think if she was into that at all it would have exhibited itself over the time that you knew her?"

"Yes."

After a rather perfunctory cross-examination by Mike Larson, Jackie Sanders is excused.

Bailey is now at the end of his witness list, except for Evelyn herself

"Your Honor, the defense has no further witnesses except for the accused. I request that court be adjourned until tomorrow morning so we can get a fresh start and hopefully get through her testimony in one day without interruption."

The prosecution voices no objection, and the court-martial goes into recess until the following morning.

WHITE SANDS COURTROOM
27 OCTOBER 1983

Outwardly, Evelyn seems relatively composed as she faces what could be the most crucial moments of her life. Bailey feels compelled to give his client as much moral and psychological support as he can before she takes the stand.

As they wait at the defense table before the judge and jury enter, Bailey tells Evelyn, "Remember, all you have to do is tell the truth. It's that simple. You have the right to give your side of this story, and the jury has been waiting to hear it. We've laid the groundwork for them to, at least, cast a good deal of doubt on Denise's version of the story."

Bailey has done everything humanly possible to make the final decision a fifty-fifty game. He knows only too well that military justice for murder-one cannot be lenient. He looks Evelyn in the eyes. "Evelyn, level with me. You haven't really told the whole story, have you? Not to the M.P.s, the police, or even me, I don't know what it is, but I can sense that you've been holding back. Not lying; it just seems to me that you haven't taken it as far as it deserves. Would I be right about that?"

Evelyn stares back at Bailey. Then, she lowers her gaze. "You already know that I want to protect Denise. I don't really know what I should do. I want to do everything I can for her."

Her voice quivers. The words now come out with difficulty. "Do I want to throw my life away doing it? I just don't know! I told her it was forever, and I meant it to be forever." Evelyn is ever so close to crying, but manages to compose herself.

Bailey pats her arm. "Evelyn. I understand how you feel, and yet I don't. I can't make the decision you have to make. It is yours and only yours to make,"

Evelyn wipes the small amount of moisture that has escaped unto her cheeks and then sits up straighter in her chair. In a trembling voice come the words, "I'm okay".

Bailey begins his final preparation of Evelyn Davis.

"I'll start you out easy with simple questions that really don't have much to do with the case. That way you'll get a chance to relax a little and get use to being on the stand. Then when we get to the nitty-gritty, you'll have a better chance of being comfortable up there. All right?"

Evelyn doesn't answer.

Bailey's hope of seeing a positive sign is extinguished.

The jurors file in and take their places, followed by Colonel Dennison.

Bailey announces, "The defense calls Specialist Davis to the stand."

Evelyn walks to the witness table, erect and with shoulders squared in the military manner. She is sworn in and takes her seat.

Bailey does as he promised and asks her a series of necessary but harmless questions: about her life, family background, growing up, her Army service and finally the circumstances of her relationship with Denise Rakes.

She tells the jury how she thought about leaving the Army and marrying Rakes.

"I had heard of two places it's legal to marry a female. I like the Army a whole lot, but I am to a point where it is like I can't really hide what I am any more. I'm not as big as a man, but I'm not a woman, either. I want to get out; I want to marry somebody who is going to come back to me and be there for me."

Bailey then takes Evelyn's story to the night of Angela Kinney's death.

Evelyn testifies that she and Kinney were at Denise Rakes' home and they were arguing heatedly about the triangle that Rakes perceived to exist among the three of them.

"I just didn't want to be there. I didn't really think— I'd never seen Denise violent before. So I left the house. I walked out the front door to a park. I sat down on the swings for a few minutes."

"How long were you outside?"

"Maybe twenty minutes or so, sir."

"Did you eventually go back inside?"

"I started back toward the house. When I got back, I opened the door and I looked toward the family room, which is where I had left Angela sitting. She wasn't there and I said, "Where's Angela?""

"Denise was sitting with her back to me on the edge of a chair in her living room and she said, 'She's gone'.""

Evelyn stops talking. There is a long moment of silence. For the first time, she looks down at her tightly clasped hands. Bailey holds his breath. *'It'll be now or never.'*

Without waiting for Bailey's next question, she begins again. Her voice is resolute. "I smelled a strong odor. When I moved closer to where Denise was sitting, I saw Angela on the floor in front of the chair with a rope around her neck. Denise had the ends of it in her hands. She said 'If you love me then you'll help me'.""

"What happ...." Bailey does not get to complete his next sentence. If there is an umbilical cord between Evelyn and her attorney, it is cut.

Evelyn continued. "I told Denise that we would have to get rid of the body. We wrapped the body in the poncho. We both picked her up. Angela was pretty heavy. We loaded the body in my car. Denise drove. I was too upset. All I could think of was that she was dead because of me."

"Denise and I went to her house and checked on the children. Then we drove off: Denise driving my car and me driving Angela Kinney's."

She continues and describes the incident in which she was stopped by the M.P.s.

"Let me take you ahead a bit. Did you eventually end up at the place where Angela was found?"

"Yes sir. Denise decided on the place. She said she knew a road that hardly anyone uses."

"What happened once you got there?"

"We both took the body out of the car and carried it down a small hill. We unrolled the body out of the poncho. Denise said nobody would see her for a couple of days and by that time she would be gone. Then we got back in and drove away."

"Now, you've heard the testimony that during that weekend and before the military police called you in to be interviewed that you allegedly make some phone calls to Angela's unit. Is that true?"

"Yes. I wanted somebody to find her. She was still somebody's. I got children. I wouldn't want to have them found five or ten days after somebody did something to them."

"Did you both come up with what you would say if you were asked about Angela?"

A long pause; but now her hands are free of each other. "Denise did, sir."

"What was the plan that she came up with?"

"She told me that if anybody asked, we'd just say we were together earlier that night and that was going to be it."

"When you were questioned at White Sands, you pretty much told them that you last saw Denise and Angela alive together in the house. Is that substantially what you said?"

"Yes sir."

"How come at that time you didn't tell them the truth?"

"I didn't want Denise to be caught, sir."

"Why not?"

Her voice betrays the flood-tide of emotions behind the wall retaining them. "Cause I loved her, sir."

"Did you realize that you might get in trouble by covering for her?"

"I loved her, sir. I can't often match men in a lot of physical things; but what I can do is protect the person I love. I was protecting her."

"When you were being questioned by the police and gave your first statement, you were concerned about Denise?"

"Yes sir."

"Yet, you already knew that she was telling on you?"

"Yes sir."

"Did you leave out the part about when you came back into the house and Denise Rakes was in the process of strangling Angela Kinney?"

"Yes sir."

"And why was that?"

"'Cause they wanted to prosecute her for murder and put her to death."

"You were willing, in essence, to risk your own hide for her?"

"I had to, sir. They were taking away my world. The Army knows I'm gay. My kids are going to be done for. I won't have Denise. It really didn't matter."

"You've come to court today and you, in essence, have now told a third version of what happened. Why is it today that you're not sticking with that second statement?"

The wall is breached. Just short of total release, her voice is that of a soul in pain. "I've another love: my two kids also need me. I love Denise; but she needs the help that I can't give her.

"Even though she's done everything she's done to you?"

She answers softly, "Yes sir."

"And even though she sat in that chair and basically said you committed murder?"

"Yes sir."

Captain Patrick J. Bailey takes a big breath. "Did you kill Angela Kinney?"

"No sir.

He quickly says, "No further questions."

At the noon break, Bailey hustles out to a nearby P.X. and brings back sandwiches and cokes. He and Evelyn eat in the courtroom. The room is deserted except for an M.P. who's keeping an eye on Evelyn. Bailey tries to prepare her for cross-examination. "You didn't hurt yourself at all. You really gave the jury a lot to think about."

"Did any of them believe me?"

Bailey grimaces a little. "That's hard to tell. You never know what a jury is thinking, especially a military jury. They take their job seriously, and aren't going to give any noticeable reaction."

"But I can tell you one thing: They were listening hard. Never moved around in their chairs or looked at their watches or anything. I think if they were restless and bored or had already made up their minds, they wouldn't have paid that close attention."

"What happens now?"

Bailey again goes over the cross-examination process. "Larson will come after you pretty strong. He'll be trying to dig out discrepancies and inconsistencies in your story. And he'll probably try to give you a hard time about telling different versions to the cops and then on the witness stand."

"I messed up, didn't I?"

"Don't worry about it. What's done is done and we can't go back and change it. Anyway, it finally came out that you were trying to protect Denise, and that ought to weigh something with the jury."

"Maybe," Evelyn says, "And maybe they'll think I was lying the whole time, back then and now in here."

"That may be so. But you've done everything you could to straighten it all out. Just remember, all you had to do is tell it like it is. Now, if you're asked a question and you don't remember something, it's okay to say so. If you don't understand something, that's okay, too; just ask him to repeat the question or ask it a different way."

He pauses for a second. "It might get hard up there. The Army has to try to break down your story. The questions are going to get tough. Try not to let it get to you. Larson's a good man: he's just doing his job."

Evelyn says grimly. "I guess I'm ready for whatever."

The cross-examination doesn't go the way Bailey predicted.

When Evelyn takes the stand again, Larson tells her he has just a few questions.

First he probes into the circumstances that brought Evelyn, Denise Rakes and Angela Kinney together at Denise's quarters the night of the killing.

Then he takes her briefly through the strangulation, not attempting to shake her story, and moves on to the disposition of Angela's body.

"Did you help Denise Rakes lay the body in the desert?"

"Yes sir."

"You testified that you didn't kill Angela Kinney"

"Yes sir."

Bailey now knows that Larson does not believe that he can make murder-one stick. He is focusing on the disposal of the body because he has a better chance of proving the accessory charge against Evelyn.

Larson continues. "Did you call the duty section at Angela Kinney's company to tell them where the body was?"

"No sir. Not to tell them: just so somebody would at least look."

"What did you tell them when you phoned?"

"I just asked for her. I still remember the terrible feeling I had after seeing Angela Kinney's body laying on the ground. Somebody's child died for flirting. I wanted somebody to find her"

"And you helped Denise Rakes take this body because you were scared and because you loved her?"

"Because I loved her, not because I was scared."

Larson asks Evelyn a few more questions to establish when she had first heard news reports that the body had been discovered; then he surprises Bailey. "I have no further questions."

Bailey, thinking it best to leave well enough alone, tells the court he has no questions on re-direct examination. But Colonel Denison does. The judge focuses, as Larson had, on what happened after Angela Kinney was killed.

"Specialist Davis, at the time you helped Mrs. Rakes move the body and drive the car off post, did you know at that time that Angela Kinney had been killed by Mrs. Rakes?"

"Yes sir."

"So you knew a crime had been committed."

"Yes sir."

"By helping move the body and by driving one of the two cars, and by helping place the body by the side of the road, were you assisting Mrs. Rakes in not being caught?"

"Yes sir."

"You testified that the reason you did it was because you loved her. Is that correct?"

"Yes sir."

Under court-martial procedures, jurors are entitled to ask questions if they want to. None do.

Bailey rests the defense case. Larson says that the Army has no further evidence.

It is still fairly early in the afternoon, but the judge adjourns court to allow a fresh start the next day on the final procedures: prosecution and defense closing arguments, the judge's instructions to the jury, and the jurors' determination of Evelyn's guilt or innocence.

WHITE SANDS COURTROOM
28 OCTOBER 1983

Today, Bailey's slept-in-it look is gone. His uniform is crisp and newly pressed. His brass and shoes are polished to a high glow.

Captain Larson takes his place in front of the jury, notes in hand. He reviews the evidence establishing that Angela Kinney had been strangled to death, and refreshes the jury's memory of the prosecution's case against Evelyn Davis.

Then he starts hammering at the point Pat Bailey had predicted would be his main platform in cross-examining Evelyn: the fact that she has given more than one version of her story.

"The accused has now made three statements which are before you, concerning the incidents surrounding Angela Kinney's death, her murder. To date, not one of those three statements matches either of the other two. It is not until she takes the stand that we first hear from the accused that she saw Denise Rakes strangling Angela Kinney. Why is this when it is obviously too late for the government to go to any effort to corroborate her statement? Why this first time? Why all of a sudden?"

Larson supplies his own answer. "She had to come up with a better story. So for the third time, she's changed her story. But she doesn't want to come up with a completely new story because some of the facts in the first two statements matched each other."

"After six months of opportunities to tell the truth she all of a sudden comes up with the so-called truth on the last possible day. This is it. This is for the whole bag of marbles. And why did she keep changing her story? The answer: "I still love Denise and want to protect her.""

Colonel Denison, who has been fidgeting noticeably through Larson's presentation, interrupts.

"Approach the bench, please."

Larson and Bailey stand in front of the judge, out of earshot of the jury. "Your argument," Denison tells Larson, "is coming perilously close to commenting about the accused's failure to make a statement during the months she's been under charges. That's improper. You can make argument that this is a different story than she's told before, but three times you have made reference to the amount of time that's expired before this statement has come up. That includes times when she's had a right not to say anything. If that happens again I may have to take steps."

He asks Bailey if he wants an instruction issued to the jury that would reinforce what he has just told Larson. "I was about to ask for a mistrial," Bailey replied. "Your cautions are, in the defense's opinion, sufficient, but we will request an instruction at the proper time."

"All right," Denison replies "Let's proceed."

After his run-in with the judge, Larson shifts course. He lays before the jury an interpretation of what happened the night of the murder.

As background, he sets up what he describes as Evelyn's motivation: "She's afraid of losing Denise Rakes, and brings Angela Kinney to Rakes' house to make Rakes jealous. But, Denise Rakes doesn't play the game. She doesn't get jealous, she doesn't get excited. She gets confused"

Then, Larson postulates that Evelyn turned on Angela Kinney. "It scared Angela. She reacted violently. She fought, she tried to leave. But by this time, the accused cannot let her leave. Angela Kinney knows too much, and she is mad that she has been used. So what does the accused think? "I'll scare Angela Kinney even more so she won't dare talk about me."

Larson states that Evelyn then tells Denise to get something with which to tie Angela up. When Angela is bound, Evelyn says she would just as soon kill both of them. "Denise is so shaken she wets herself; and is in no condition to come to Angela's aid as Evelyn puts the rope around her neck and strangles her. Then Davis makes Denise Rakes help her dispose of the body in the desert, threatening that if she doesn't help, Evelyn will implicate her in the murder.

The prosecutor builds to his conclusion. "You will not sit in judgment of Denise Rakes, though you may want to, though I may wish that you would. She's not here. We've got to leave the civilians to mete out justice to Denise Rakes because they have all this evidence also.

There can be no other conclusion. The accused set up Angela Kinney and murdered her, for whatever reason. She murdered her and then dumped her body in the desert."

'*Not a bad job*', Bailey thinks to himself as Larson takes his seat. '*He did the best he could with what he had.*'

Bailey stands and begins his own closing statement to the jury.

"There are three people on trial, not two. One: obviously, Specialist Davis. Two: obviously, Denise Rakes. Three: Angela Kinney. She's dead, she's buried, but she is in this room and she's laid out before you and she's staring you in the face and she's saying to you, 'I was not stupid. I was not so dumb. Don't let Denise Rakes do more harm to me than she's already done. Listen to what Denise Rakes said. Don't think just because you have a copy of her statement she's telling the truth.'"

Point by point, Bailey recounts Rakes' testimony for the jury, refuting each item with an argument based on Evelyn's version of the story, physical evidence such as the layout of Rakes' quarters where Kinney died.

Then, zeroing in on Rakes' overall credibility, Bailey asks the jurors to consider the calm, dispassionate manner in which she has testified, suggesting that if events had transpired the way she said they had and had shocked her to the extent she claimed, could she have been so devoid of emotion when she revisited that night in her testimony?

"I submit to you that anyone witnessing a murder as Denise Rakes indicated, where she was so upset that it caused her to wet her pants in fright, is going to relive that if she testifies about it. She's not going to sit on that witness stand matter-of-factly describing blow-by-blow without the least little bit of emotion.

Think about it. Could you describe such a traumatic event to a roomful of strangers and not even quiver your lip at least one time? Not once? Not even show a single, little, tiniest amount of remorse or sadness? She's cold-blooded."

He recounts how each defense witness had destroyed a piece of Rakes' story, and emphasizes Dr. Chapin's analysis of Evelyn as a person who would go to any length to avoid violence.

"He described for you the type of person who might do that, someone with a personality disorder. It would take that kind of person to commit what has been described as a violent, bizarre crime. Who did he describe?"

"Is there any one of us who would want to be convicted on this evidence? Would any one of us feel fairly judged if we were sent to prison on the state of the evidence in this case? The answer is no!"

Now, Bailey deliberately walks within an arms-length of the jury. In a subdued, but firm voice, he says, "For a brief moment, I want you to forget all that you have learned about this murder and answer this question: Haven't you been listening to a tragic love story: a love story between, not two women, but a man and a woman? A love so intense that it caused the woman to kill and the man to act to protect? Then, walk in the man's shoes and answer a second question: if the woman that you swore to love forever did something terrible, yet logical in the terms of her own psychopathology, what would you do to protect that love?"

Bailey lets silence dominate the moment before continuing. "This a love story so intense that it caused one to commit a crime of passion and the other, at peril of death, to protect her."

"You don't have to please me with your verdict; you don't have to please Specialist Davis or the government. You don't have to please the military judge or any of the people who've been following this trial. The only thing you have to please is your own conscience.

Sometimes you really have to look below the surface of things to avoid a horrible tragedy. In this case, it would be a horrible tragedy to send that young woman to prison for something she hasn't done and what she did do to protect the woman he loves."

There is no missing the emphasis on the word, HE.

Bailey sits down. Evelyn looks at him. Her eyes are water.

Larson offers a rebuttal argument that seeks to undo some of the damage Bailey's closing has done to the Army's case, but he cannot introduce any new material.

Bailey can sense from the jurors' body language that they are restless with the repetition and want to get on with their part in the case.

The judge apparently thinks so too. Turning to the jury, he addresses a question to Colonel James A. Chernault, its president (foreman, in civilian parlance). "It's nearly eleven hundred hours and my instructions probably will take about an hour. Do you want to continue now or wait until after lunch?"

Chernault doesn't hesitate. "If it's all right with the other parties, Your Honor, we'd like to receive instructions now and begin our deliberations after the noon break."

"Very well. Does either side have any trouble with that?"

Larson and Bailey indicate they have no objection. Denison turns again to the jury. His instructions are mostly standard, covering elements of the offenses charged, the proof necessary to find premeditation, the difference between direct and circumstantial evidence, and the definition of reasonable doubt.

The nature of the testimony requires the addition of instructions as to the nature of duress, which Evelyn claimed as a reason for helping dispose of the body; the definition of an accomplice, and standards by which to consider testimony that Rakes gave under a grant of immunity from prosecution.

The judge reminds the jurors that four of the five of them will have to concur in a guilty verdict and again admonishes them not to discuss the case with anyone. He taps his gavel to signal that it is lunchtime.

Before, the courtroom M.P.s can lead Evelyn back to her cell, in a low voice she whispers to Bailey "Can you guess what's going to happen?"

Bailey shakes his head.

Evelyn returns to her cell and Bailey is left to have a solitary, thoughtful lunch at the Officers' Club.

The court-martial reconvenes at 1 p.m. and is in session only long enough for the judge to formally turn the evidence over to the jurors and discharge them to begin their deliberations in a conference room adjacent to the court.

As they shuffle their notes and documents together, cleaning house to await the verdict, Bailey asks Mike Larson if he can ask him a personal question.

"Sure," the prosecutor said. "I don't think we can do any damage to each other at this point."

"I was just wondering," Bailey said, "if you've been getting the same vibrations about this case as I have."

"What kind of vibrations would those be?"

"It's like somebody's in a big hurry here, I'm thinking that the Army really doesn't want to deal with the elements of homosexuality, especially publicly like this, and wants to get this over as quickly as possible. I'm wondering if that's why they jumped on Rakes' bandwagon and decided to make a case against my client based only on her statements."

Larson considers his response for a moment. "I don't think I should answer that. We might be talking about mistrial, misconduct, miscarriage of justice . . . whatever. I was assigned this case when it was developed enough to take it to trial. It went through federal court and I presume was thoroughly reviewed at every level that matters in the Army and among the civilian authorities,"

He pauses. "Having said that, there are a couple things I can tell you. I've heard through the grapevine that there are people here on post and in the El Paso P.D. who have the same misgivings you have. I understand that the provost marshal, Mark Silverstine, and one of the El Paso detectives in the case, Ray Martinez, have been watching this thing closer than they would most other cases. What that means, I can't say. But for whatever it's worth, there it is."

Bailey isn't surprised. He has seen Martinez in the courtroom on more than one occasion and from what his few contracts with Colonel Silverstine, he can visualize him watching and maybe, just maybe, pulling more than a few strings.

He and Larson return to their offices to await the verdict. Bailey spends the afternoon preparing what he will need to plead for the lightest sentence possible for Evelyn should she be convicted.

Bailey is still in his office at 6 p.m. when the clerk of the court-martial phones to tell him that the jury is coming back in. He hurries to the courtroom and joins Evelyn at the defense table. She had been brought from jail a few minutes earlier. The jurors are already seated.

Judge Denison enters and takes his place, joined by Mike Larson and the other court personnel.

Denison turns to the jury. "Colonel Chernault, has the court arrived at findings?"

"The court has Your Honor."

He hands the written verdict to the clerk, who takes it to the judge. Denison reads the verdict silently; then returns it to Chernault.

Denison addresses Evelyn. "Specialist Davis, please present yourself to the president of the court."

Evelyn stands, faces the jury and comes to attention.

Colonel Chernault reads the findings to her. "Specialist 4 Evelyn C. Davis, it is my duty as president of this court to inform you that the court, in closed session and upon secret written ballot with two-thirds of the members present at the time the vote was taken, concurring in each finding of guilty, has found you:

Of the specification of and Charge I, murder in the first degree, not guilty.

Of the specification of and Charge II, accessory to murder in the first degree, guilty."

Prompted by the judge, Evelyn salutes the president of the court and returns to her place at the defense table. Before court adjourns until the next morning, when she will be sentenced on the accessory conviction, she has a few moments with Bailey.

He grins broadly and shakes her hand. "You did it. You told the truth and it came through loud and clear."

Evelyn's face relaxes for the first time and the little smile that Bailey has been patiently awaiting for finally emerges. "Yes, but I'm guilty on the second charge. What will they do to me?"

"Evelyn," Bailey said, "I think we both knew—everybody here knew—that you'd probably lose on that charge. It was hard to avoid. You did go with Denise to get rid of the body. You and I know why, and maybe the jury does, too. But what happened, happened and they couldn't get around it even if they want to."

He pats her arm.

"I figure you'll maybe get a little jail time, but I don't know. I'll talk it down as much as I can. You'll be discharged and everything else that goes with that, but you were ready to get out anyway, right?"

"Yes. After everything that's happened there's no way I'd stay in the Army, even if they wanted me. I can't pretend to be somebody I'm not any more. I just want to do what I have to do and go home to my kids."

"They're in good hands up in Omaha," Bailey said. "It might be a while before you can be with them, but at least, they'll know that their mother ..." Bailey stops and then quickly corrects himself. "Their father is coming back."

WHITE SANDS COURTROOM
29 OCTOBER 1983

Colonel Denison explains the sentencing procedure to the jurors. The defense will present evidence in mitigation, then both sides will give brief arguments before the jury retires to fix the terms of Evelyn's punishment.

Bailey calls five witnesses. Four were Evelyn's former supervisors and colleagues at the White Sands health clinic, who testified unanimously and unreservedly as to her competence, diligence, dependability and personal characteristics of compassion and dedication to healing.

The fifth witness is Paul Riley, one of Evelyn's older brothers. He tells the court of her children's stay in Omaha, stressing that they seemed confused and afraid. "They need their mother."

Then Bailey calls Evelyn to the stand.

As he had promised, she is there only a few minutes.

First, Bailey has her outline her Army career as a medical lab technician and operating room assistant. Then he introduces a letter he had received from Evelyn's mother, Cecilia, written before her death: "Captain Bailey, this is not an easy letter for me to write, simply because of its importance. I want so badly to be helpful for my daughter's sake. We had a few turbulent years from which she emerged no longer a caterpillar, but a lovely butterfly. I am proud of her stamina and ability to survive and stand tall even under adverse conditions. This testifies to me of a person who has strength of character and faith in God, one who feels loved and full of self-worth. These are my feelings."

Next Bailey produces a letter Evelyn had written to Cecilia on Mother's Day in 1979 which reads in part: "Your Mother's Day wish has always been to save your children's souls. Well, my time is nearing. I know because of the things that are happening in my life. You will live in the hearts of those whose lives you have touched for as long as they live and maybe even longer."

"Now I know this isn't much, but it's all I have to offer this year. I'm not good at writing, but you are a very special woman in my life."

He also presents portions of a poem Evelyn had written for Cecilia on a Mother's Day two years later: "Throughout the years you've always been there before we knew it, to lend a hand before we asked for it, and you've given motherly love when we needed it most. So now it's time for your children to join together and take a stand, The next time you reach out for help we will all be there to lend a hand. Since birth you've doubled as a guardian angel and guiding light, so if you ever need a good talk or a cry, call your children and together we'll help you get through a long night. We love you."

"Happy Mother's Day."

Bailey is done, but the judge addresses one question to Evelyn. "If you are asked to, would you voluntarily testify in a trial involving Denise Rakes?"

"Yes sir."

Evelyn steps down.

Larson leads off the counter-arguments "Angela Kinney is dead. We can't bring her back, but does she not cry from the grave and ask for justice?

. Would she not want appropriate punishment for that person who held up the wheels of justice for so long, and helped and assisted in leaving her body out in the desert to be found by two garbage men?"

He notes the evidence Bailey has presented that revealed the love between Evelyn and her late mother and the bond between Evelyn and her children.

"What about Angela Kinney's family? Did they not love Angela Kinney? Would they not have wanted to see something better come of her life and her death than to be thrown out in the desert in the middle of the night like garbage?"

He closes with a plea to the jury to impose a sentence that would uphold the seriousness of the accessory charge.

In his turn before the jury, Bailey is blunt and direct. "The reason why justice has not occurred in this case is because an employee of the United States government decided to charge the wrong person with murder. The reason why justice is not done in this case is because the murderer, Denise Rakes, to this day walks the streets of El Paso, free."

"I submit to you the reason Specialist Davis was an accessory after the fact to Denise Rakes' murder of Angela Kinney is for all the reasons that you've seen and heard from people who knew her. She loved too much. She cared too much. She gave of herself too much. Even when it got down to risking jail she wasn't selfish. She didn't think about her own skin. She didn't think about herself at all. She thought of somebody else who in her mind was ill, if not crazy, and she decided to help her."

He asks the jury to consider the punishment already inflicted on his client. "She stands convicted. It's not going to go away. She now has a federal criminal record forever, the rest of her life. In a lot of places that's going to affect her civil rights. Certainly it's going to affect her in terms of any clearance she might need to hold a job. Throughout the rest of her life she's going to have to deal with this in her own mind."

"This is not something that was put on to fool you. This is the saddest case you are ever going to see in your military careers. That's why you have an option of no punishment. The maximum sentence is for the Denise Rakes's of the world, not for the Evelyn Davis's. Thank you."

Emotionally wrung out from his presentation, Captain Patrick Bailey sinks into his chair. Evelyn scribbles a message on the legal pad: 'You were great. Thanks.'

Judge Denison instructs the jury on sentencing guidelines and cautions members as to what and what not they should consider in arriving at a verdict. He sends the jury off to its deliberation room; Evelyn goes back to her cell, and the other participants in the trial scatter to find a way to kill time while they wait for the verdict.

Bailey goes to the closest P.X. and has a cup of coffee. He senses that the jury wouldn't take long, and hopes that members would impose either no sentence on Evelyn or one short enough to satisfy minimum demands of justice.

He is right about the time. He barely finished his coffee before the clerk began telephoning the attorneys and other participants to inform them the jury is about to return to the courtroom.

"Please be seated," Colonel Denison says when everyone is in place. "Court will come to order."

"Colonel Chernault, has the court arrived at a sentence?"

Chernault indicates that it has.

"Specialist Davis," the Judge says. "Present yourself to the president of the court, please."

Again Evelyn stands, turns toward the jury panel and salutes.

Chernault reads the sentencing document: "Specialist 4 Evelyn C. Davis, the court, in closed session and upon secret written ballot, at least two-thirds of the members present when the vote was taken concurring, sentences you:

"To be reduced to the grade of E-1; to be confined at hard labor for two years; to forfeit all pay and allowances; to be discharged from the service with a bad conduct discharge. During the time of your imprisonment, to receive whatever medical and psychological assistance is available."

With that, Evelyn's legal travail is ended.

When she has taken her seat, Colonel Denison asks, "Does the accused wish to keep the record open at this time for the possible filing of an appeal?"

Bailey stands. "Your Honor, my client and I have discussed this matter and have concluded that we will abide by the decisions of this court."

Considering what the outcome could have been, life in prison for murder or 10 years on the accessory conviction, Evelyn and Bailey had agreed to appeal only if she were convicted of murder or given an excessive sentence on the accessory charge. Two years, which no doubt would be reduced by time off for good behavior, is an acceptable result.

"Very well, then," the judge said. "The accused will remain in the custody of the provost marshal at White Sands Missile Range, pending her transfer to the federal penitentiary at Fort Leavenworth, Kansas, for execution of sentence."

He thanks the jurors for their service and announces, "There being no further matters before this court, it is adjourned."

Bailey and Larson shake hands and exchange compliments on the conduct of the trial.

Respectfully, Evelyn's M.P. holds back. With tears in her eyes, Evelyn says, "I hope you know there isn't any way I can thank you enough. You've given me my life back. In the beginning, I didn't understand you. Later, I thought that you were very smart; but today, you were better than Perry Mason."

"No," Bailey chuckles. "I was just doing my job. I couldn't have done it without such a great client."

As the M.P.s approach, Evelyn turns to accompany them. Then she hesitates, stops, and turns once more to Bailey. "You told me at the beginning that you'd call me Evelyn. From now on, you can call me Bandit, 'cause that's who I am."

Bandit Riley and Captain Pat Bailey share an unmilitary hug.

Based upon the recommendations of Captains Ellis and Chapman, the United States Army formally recognized Evelyn Davis to be Bandit Riley, man. He is sentenced to serve his prison time at Fort Leavenworth, Kansas as a male.

FORT LEAVENWORTH, KANSAS
18 AUGUST 1984

Sergeant-Major Robert Miller takes two steps into the room and comes to attention. "Sir, we have a problem."

Without looking up from the papers on his desk, Colonel James Fitzroy responds. "Same problem?"

"Yes sir."

"At ease, Sergeant. What is it this time?"

"Well, sir, we've done everything you ordered: no cellmate, only supervised activities, semi-isolation. Everything short of solitary confinement."

He pauses and shakes his head. "But Colonel, you know we don't really run this prison. The trustees and old hands do. They have more to say about what happens with Riley than we do. They even auction off trapping rights on the son of a bitch, or the bitch, or whatever they call him/her. Now he or she is in the infirmary again. I'll say one thing, he fights pretty good. But when it's three or four to one, there's one guaranteed loser."

"How bad?" the colonel asks.

"Not much worse than the last time," Miller replied. "Cuts and bruises, a helluva shiner - maybe a broken rib or two. But if this keeps up, somebody's gonna get hurt bad - or maybe killed. You put a woman, or half a woman, or whatever Riley is, in with a bunch of male prisoners, that's just a disaster waiting to happen."

Fitzroy nods. "I know, Sergeant, I know. You and your men have done the best you could. None of us asked for this. We can handle murderers, rapists, arsonists, you name it. But, this one..... Anyway, I've just got some good news for both of us."

He opens a file on his desk and consults the stilted military wording. "This just came in this morning. It's from Fifth Army, and what it does is take this Riley character off our hands."

Miller brightens noticeably. "He's getting out, sir?"

"Not quite," the colonel said. "But it appears that because of some pretty hard lobbying from outside, an Army medical board has decided that Ms. or Mr. Riley has a physical condition that amounts to being a man trapped in a woman's body. And since what we imprison here are bodies, this one goes to the women's section and that means right now!"

Miller is incredulous. "The Army said that? I thought that stuff was just a bunch of bullshit."

"Not necessarily," the colonel answers. "And even if it is, I don't care whether it's pure bullshit or a 100 percent straight word. It gets this him or her out of here."

Miller comes to attention again and salutes. "Sir, that's the best news I've heard in a long time."

"That's for damn sure, Sergeant. You're dismissed. Have a nice day."

"It's a nice day already, Colonel," Miller says on his way out.

Then, Colonel Fitzroy calls his counterpart on the female side of Leavenworth prison on the telephone. "Janet, I'm sending you over a set of orders, a big, thick file, and one warm body. Before they get there, you need to take an aspirin and two slugs of vodka. And don't call me in the morning."

The same day, Bandit Riley is taken in shackles from Level C of the "Castle" to the women's section of the federal prison at Fort Leavenworth.

Bandit's processing goes smoothly until uniform issue when he is handed a skirt. The ensuing confrontation requires the intervention of both Colonel Janet Morehouse, the women's prison commandant, and Colonel Fitzroy.

FORT LEAVENWORTH, KANSAS
5 JANUARY 1985

Colonel Fitzroy is amused by the document sent him for his endorsement by Colonel Jane Morehouse. *'Didn't take long.'*

The cover letter states the reasons the women's commandant believes that Bandit Riley is qualified for parole after serving less than a year of his two-year sentence. 'He had been a model prisoner (despite sexual involvement with several inmates and possibly one female

M.P.), offering convincing evidence of rehabilitation. His unusual sexual orientation, even if officially recognized and certified by the Army, has proved to be a disturbing factor in both men's and women's divisions of Leavenworth and could be judged to be detrimental to the maintenance of order and discipline.'

'He has been receiving, under the directives of the medical board, regular injections of the male hormone, testosterone, and is responding to the treatment.'

And finally, Morehouse has written, 'Prisoner Riley's early release is justified (under that historic catch-all consideration) for the good of the Service.'

Fitzroy agreeing with all these findings, immediately signs off on the parole. He orders a clerk to type up an endorsement for him to sign, then looks through the rest of Bandit's parole papers.

There are letters from Bandit's attorney, Patrick Bailey, and an M.P. colonel at White Sands Missile Range named Mark Silverstine. Another letter from the prosecuting attorney at Bandit's court-martial states that the Judge Advocate General's Corps will not issue a directive or opinion in the matter.

Omaha, Nebraska
5 April 1999

In a civil service performed at City Hall in Omaha, Nebraska, Pauline Thomas accepted in marriage Cecilia's HER's T-shirt from Bandit Riley.

Epilogue

"Bandit" is based upon a true story.

At gestational age of five weeks, Evelyn Riley became "Bandit" Riley when her mother received male hormones to ward off a threatened miscarriage.

Evelyn Davis became "Bandit" Riley courtesy of the U.S. Army that, yielding to expert testimony, came to accept that a man had been imprisoned in a woman's body.

In recognizing the potential that mis-sex imprinting can occur *in utero*, the U.S. Army demonstrated a level of understanding and compassion that society has yet to reach more than two decades later.